Sample Excerpts

…Munson screamed at that yellow flag. "That dastardly flag. That awful, terrible color is on the green grass now—that yellow flag is going to wipe this play out, and we're right back to where we began, and we've got no hope at all again, and it's all because of that dastardly flag. That yellow color on the green grass has just dashed Georgia's hopes." We all sat back down. The flag just took the air out of that stadium. The stadium went from shaking one minute on the Georgia side to deathly quiet the next minute. I've never seen such a swing of emotion. Munson captured it perfectly.…

…Lindsay caught the ball and ran for a touchdown to beat Florida. This was before the remodeling on the Gator Bowl. Munson said, "Well, the stadium's gonna collapse now." Then he talked about condos up in St. Simons, "There's going to be some property destroyed tonight." In my lifetime, that was probably the greatest description of one play.…

…I've been blessed to broadcast all these years. I'd like to thank the fans and say, "God bless you," because they're something. The game is supposed to be for the fans. I wish there was something we could do to make it easier to park, easier to find places to tailgate. These are wonderful fans here. Make no mistake about that. This is a real good bunch here.…

Sample Excerpts From This Book

...Erk Russell said the boy got caught with a girl in his room. Erk called all the players up and said, "I've got some good news, and I've got some bad news. What do you want to hear first?" They said, "We want to hear the bad news." He said, "Well, so and so got caught with a girl in his room, and he's going to have to be punished for it." They said, "What's the good news, Coach?" He said, "The good news is that if he can get a girl in his room, any of y'all can." I said, "How did you know they were going to ask for the bad news first?" He said, "They always ask for the bad news first."...

...Georgia football season actually falls on the opening day of dove season. Everybody in the field would have their radios tuned in to the Georgia game so you could hear Munson wherever you were out there. I've just got to believe that some of those doves must now be Bulldog fans!...

...The first time I went to Jacksonville, I didn't have a ticket. My dad had given me a nice Callaway driver, and out of desperation, I traded it to my dad's best friend for a set of club-level seats. Going to Alltel Stadium and being able to sit in the club level was huge! Using fairway irons for tee shots on the long holes is tough, though....

For GEORGIA FANS ONLY!

To Herb
Go Dawgs ?!!
Don Sullivan

PETER MOKHIBER
DON SULLIVAN
RICH WOLFE

This book is not affiliated with or endorsed by the University of Georgia or the NCAA.

Published by Rich Wolfe and Lone Wolfe Press, a division of Richcraft. Distribution, marketing, publicity, interviews, and book signings handled by Wolfegang Marketing Systems Ltd.—But Not Very.

The author, Rich Wolfe, can be reached at 602-738-5889.

International Standard Book Number: 978-0-9800978-1-8

Printed in the United States of America

10 9 8 7 6 5 4 3 2 1

Photos provided by, and used with permission of Rich Wolfe, *Sports Illustrated,* and the individuals whose stories appear in this book.

Cover design: Joe Suggs
Cover art: Aaron Jones
Interior design: The Printed Page, Phoenix AZ.
Author's Agent: T. Roy Gaul

Dedication

To:

Rita and Connie
—D.S. and P.M.

Dee and Jimmy Matthews of Albany, GA—
Two great Bulldog fans, two great people
—R.W.

Acknowledgments

We would like to pass a huge thank you to those without whom we could not have produced this book. Major thanks to Roger Roemmich and Kari March for introducing us to many of the marvelous people in the university community interviewed in the book. To Anne Sweaney who knows just about everybody and put up with my constant calls! And to Skip Balcomb, the first person we met in Athens at the Hill Top Grille, who provided us with a long list of great people to interview. To Wingate Downs, well known Athens and former UGA photographer, who provided access to his years of photography as well as his portfolio. He really does own a Poulan Weedeater. To Joe Suggs who contributed his story as well as his artistic talent and provided the cover art. His contribution was gigantic and is greatly appreciated. To Aaron Jones who gave us access to his massive collection of programs and tickets as well as his keen eye for anything Red and Black. He and Joe are authorities on Georgia football and made sure that we did not go astray with our facts. To Corky Coleman who really knows that the ACC is a weak conference. To Jim Belliveau, who wishes he had gone to Georgia. To Danielle whose son Christian is a sure shot future Bulldog linebacker. To TWB, the Round Man, who would have been pleased to add another Georgia book to his library. And last, but especially, to all those wonderful people who love this great university so much.

Thanks also to two women who worked behind the scenes to make this book a reality, Ellen Brewer in Edmond, Oklahoma, and Lisa Liddy at The Printed Page in Phoenix, Arizona.

Preface

Last summer I was having a beer in Marietta with an old classmate of mine, Rich Wolfe. Actually, I was having a beer and he was watching and talking. He was telling me about all the fun he had over the last several years writing sports books. He told how many he had written and, indeed, he may be the most prolific producer of sports books in America and, just maybe, in the world. He was talking about books to come and future ventures and I immediately interrupted him and told him he should consider doing Georgia next. He changed the subject, but I was persistent. Just to shut me up, he told me that I should do the Georgia book and he would guide me through it. Well, that was a ridiculous notion and I deflected that idea in a hurry. Rich then became the aggressor and began to tell me how much fun doing a sports book was and how many truly interesting Georgia fans I would meet. I told him I would think about it. Well, I talked to a friend, Peter Mokhiber, a huge SEC fan, and just like that, we were on board. We found out in a hurry that there is a lot of work that goes into something like this but, man, has it ever been fun!

I became a Georgia fan many years ago by default—I don't like Georgia Tech! But then, my son Chris went to Georgia and the real fun began. My wife learned what an "upsidedown Margarita" was and it was football in Athens from then on. Chris has since graduated and now we torment him during football season by going to Georgia games while he is stuck in a dingy "game watch" bar with hundreds of other out of state Dawgs in Virginia. My wife and I have met a good number of our son's friends who were tailgaters just like us so we always have people to party with at home games. But, after doing this book, all those other Bulldog fans have become personalities to me. Not the people we interviewed but all those other Bulldog fans. Now I see people wearing the Red and Black and I want to interview them. I know that there are stories at every game just begging to be told and emotions brought on by memories of hot September

Saturdays or cool November breezes that can bring tears to the eyes of the hardest fan. We love meeting our daughter Kerry on Saturdays at the games so we can give her gas money and see her and her Delta Zeta sisters all dressed up for the games. Soon she will graduate from college and it will be just the two of us and our new family of 92,000!

Peter and I always look forward to travel outside of the SEC and the opportunity to engage folks in debates regarding the strength of the SEC. As any knowledgeable fan knows, they always lose. But there is more. We now include a compelling argument that the SEC has the best fans, too.

As I write this, another promising season is underway but I don't feel any different. I begin every season feeling that, with a couple of breaks here, and some good bounces there, and with lots of hard work, this year's team can win the SEC and maybe, just maybe, the whole enchilada!

These stories were really fun to collect. Some of them were still fun after I had read them for the third and fourth time during proofing. I hope you enjoy them and maybe they will even stir some memories that you can relate to us for volume II.

—Don Sullivan

Chat Rooms

Chapter 1

Turn Your Radio On

I've Never Met Larry Munson, But I've Known Him All My Life

HAPPY TRAILS TO A CHOICE VOICE

Larry Munson

Larry Munson, 86, one of the best loved sportscasters in the business has just ended a 55-year career in broadcasting topped off with over 40 years as the voice of the Georgia Bull-dogs. His calls are played by fans everywhere and will be for as long as there is Georgia football. He defines the term 'homer' and makes it fun. A tailgater at the "blackout game" put it best; "Even people who "hate" him love him!

I don't know if I would have gone into sportscasting if I hadn't fought in the war. I heard a commercial on the radio for radio broadcasting school. The cost was $200. That's what my discharge pay was. You had to spend 13 weeks in class, and then they promised you a job at a radio station. That commercial was the reason I went into radio. I had never given it a lot of thought, but when I heard that the commercial, and it fit the two-hundred bucks I had in my pocket, I signed up.

When I came out of the class, I wound up in Wyoming where a guy named Curt Gowdy was getting ready to leave. Gowdy and I became friends. He's the one who told me to get in baseball so I could make some money. Gowdy went to Oklahoma City and then to the Red Sox. I took a job with a minor league baseball team in Nashville, Tennessee.

I was on a major station that had a big signal in Nashville. Some people from the Gardner Advertising Agency in St. Louis were listening. They had been listening to me for two years, and I didn't realize it. When the Braves decided to move out of **MILWAUKEE***, these guys from St. Louis hired an announcer out of Chicago, and took me as the second one. That's how I wound up coming to Atlanta with the Braves.

My first day in spring training, the University of Georgia announcer left to do the Falcons on Channel 5. This put Georgia in a hole. The Georgia athletic director and I were close friends. I called him when I heard about the opening, and I had the job before I ever went to spring training that first day. Before I had interviewed a ballplayer, I had another job.

> I don't know if I would have gone into sportscasting if I hadn't fought in the war.

I'm not sure how the fans took to me in the early days, getting adjusted to my style as compared to Ed Thilenius. Ed had a heck of a voice, a sensational network-caliber voice. And he had many fans. I was what you call a 'homer.' I pulled too much to win. Everything was 'us' and 'we.' A lot of people didn't go for that, in particular, members of the press. That was just what I did and always have done.

I also had a job in Atlanta. I was tied up so often, I hardly ever got to Athens. But I picked up Vince Dooley's coach's call-in show. I got to know Dooley pretty well, since I would come over one day a week and sit and talk with him. Dooley was the head coach, and I was just a young announcer, so we didn't have a close relationship. But, he took me under his wing a little bit, in a subtle way.

I'd drive over from Atlanta on Tuesdays during practice. When he saw me coming, he would step off the practice field, and we would

---

*In the movie "Naked Gun" two prominent police officers were named Officer Adcock and Officer Mathews. The producers, David and Jerry Zucker loved Joe Adcock and Eddie Mathews when the Zuckers were growing up in **MILWAUKEE**. Eddie Mathews is the only Brave to play for the Boston, Milwaukee and Atlanta Braves.

walk around together while he answered anything I asked. I wasn't making tapes or anything. He just told me everything that happened, and what the injury situation was. Meanwhile, the players were scrimmaging behind us while we walked. After practice, he and Barbara would have me over to their house for supper.

Erk Russell was in charge of getting the opposing team's film. He would let me look at the offense film so that by the time the game came on Saturday, I had seen every play the other team had run the week before. That helped me a lot since I didn't have much time to spend in Athens.

Erk and I shared fishing stories. I remember his frustration when he started to play golf. He had the same experience with golf that **TED WILLIAMS*** of the Red Sox had. He couldn't hit the damn ball and he couldn't understand why! It just about killed him. He put his fishing tackle away, determined to master golf. That's about the way Williams went, too, only Williams never put his fishing tackle away.

In those days I did an awful lot of **BOWLS***. Texaco assigned me to the Gator Bowl, the Bluebonnet Bowl, the Liberty Bowl and the Sun Bowl. I did those four every year. Back then you weren't allowed to do your own school. The big networks were in control of the Rose, the Cotton and the Orange Bowls, so I was doing second-tier bowls, to tell you the truth. I was traveling alone. I've done a lot of traveling alone my whole life, as it's turned out.

I don't know how you come up with particular phrases that stick with people; it just happens. People tell me that I said something strange, funny or odd. But, in 41 years, there have only been ten of them, so that's like one call every four years. There haven't been that many funny calls.

*Former astronaut and Senator John Glenn was Ted Williams' squadron leader in Korea. TED WILLIAMS was John Glenn's wing man.

*In all the 1950s there were never more than nine BOWL games annually compared to three times that amount today.

"Run Lindsay," was one. Up at Tennessee a few years ago the 'hob-nail boot' thing came out of nowhere. Nobody plans those things. I've heard announcers planning things. You can tell, if you're an announcer, if some guy's going to fake something. The "hob-nail boot' game in Knoxville, Tennessee sticks out as special because we won the game, and it's tough to beat Tennessee at Knoxville.

We've had some things happen since Coach Richt got here that were unusual. We won major games, and we won a championship. It's hard now, everything's changed, the rules, the academic rules, and it's still changing. I don't know where it's all going.

> I'd like to thank the fans and say, "God bless you," because they're something.

I worry more than most announcers, I always have. I drove Dooley nuts, he said. I was constantly worried that we didn't have the same type of material and didn't have the speed the opposition had. I would give him the devil about it.

I don't know how much longer I'll be doing the games, maybe another couple of years. There's no way of telling. Age is involved now, and it hasn't been involved before. Physical health is involved, and that hasn't been involved before either.

I'd like to thank the fans and say, "God bless you," because they're something. I know that all the rules have changed, tailgating has changed, and it's harder now to find a place to cook and have parties before and during the game. I'm sorry for that. The game is supposed to be for the fans. I wish there was something we could do to make it easier to park, easier to find places to tailgate. These are wonderful fans here. Make no mistake about that. This is a real good bunch here.

*Following the 2008 Georgia-Central Michigan game, Munson decided that calling even home games was taking too much of a toll on him and he announced his retirement as The Voice of the Georgia Bulldogs.

I SAW IT ON THE RADIO

John Herring

Herring, 33, is a developer and an outrageous Bulldog fan from Milledgeville, Georgia. He tempers his fanatic ways with his dedication to the Fellowship of Christian Athletes.

When I was a little boy, Bear Bryant was huge in the South and all over the nation. Somebody gave me an Alabama jersey for Christmas when I was three years old. I ran around the house wearing that jersey, and my father said, "I'm going to fix this." He took me to watch Georgia play Vanderbilt the day Herschel ran for five touchdowns. That's my earliest memory. After that...I never saw that Alabama jersey again. It has been all Georgia ever since.

Georgia football season actually falls on the opening day of dove season, which is a huge thing here in the South, especially in my area where a lot of guys are hunters. I would go with my dad hunting, and everybody in the field would have their radios tuned in to the Georgia game so you could hear Munson wherever you were out there. I've just got to believe that some of those doves must now be Bulldog fans!

> Georgia football season actually falls on the opening day of dove season...

My mother's side of the family was all for Tech. As a matter of fact, the business school at Tech was named after one of my cousins on my mother's side. For us, it has always been a big rivalry. New fans will tell you stories about Florida, but old fans will always say Tech is the big rival. During the war, Tech claimed victories even though we didn't play any games. Later we didn't play games for five years because of riots in the streets after games. Some of the calls we lost by in the late eighties and nineties were terrible. Munson would rarely "bad-talk" the officiating, but when he did, he'd let them have it.

The first time I went to Jacksonville for a game, I didn't have a ticket. A lot of golfers, including friends of my dad's, go down for the game. They've all got season tickets. My dad had given me a nice Callaway driver, and out of desperation, I traded it to my dad's best friend for a set of club-level seats. Going to Alltel Stadium and being able to sit in the club level was huge! Using fairway irons for tee shots on the long holes is tough, though.

> Georgia has always been known for its beautiful women, but they say they grow Miss Americas at Ole Miss.

I'd always heard about The Grove at Ole Miss, but until you've been there, you can't fully appreciate it. Georgia has always been known for its beautiful women, but they say they grow Miss Americas at Ole Miss. When we went to The Grove, people were like **ANTS***—thousands of people crammed into this five-10 acre grove of trees. We stood there for about an hour with our mouths hanging open. It was the most unbelievable thing I'd ever seen. They break out the linen and the silver and the china. All the girls are dressed to the nines. It's definitely an experience everybody has got to enjoy at least once in their lifetime....

I used to work with Bank of America in their mortgage department. There was a lady, probably 67-68 years old, and she was a die-hard Georgia fan. She'd been going to games since she was a little girl. Her family came in with the campers on Wednesday before every game—that sort of thing. She liked to party. Well, she had this tampon box—remember this lady's almost 70 years old—and she emptied the tampons out and put those little airline bottles of liquor in the tampon box. They check you pretty good when you go into the stadium. They look through women's

***ANTS** are allergic to white chalk and are never found on football, soccer and baseball fields.

purses, especially now with security as tight as it is. I wondered how someone could still drink through the game. She said, "Come with me. We'll go through the gate, and I'll show you." Sure enough, the security woman looked through her purse, saw that tampon box, and let her right in with four or five airline bottles of liquor in her purse.

Nick Saban is one of the greatest college coaches of all-time. I think that I'm quoting him correctly on that.

THE WRITE GUY WROTE
THE WRONG STUFF

Mike Floyd

Floyd, 36, is the director of sales for Morris national magazines, the sporting group. They publish Gray's Sporting Journal, American Angler *and* Saltwater Fly Fishing *magazines among others.*

I live in Augusta, Georgia now, but I grew up in Spartanburg, South Carolina, and, as a Georgia fan it was easy to dislike Clemson. When I was a student, I was a beat runner for *The Red & Black*, covering Georgia football. We swapped stories with a rival's paper. They would write one in our paper saying bad things about us. We would write one in their paper saying bad things about them. These stories would always be posted on the Friday before the game. I finished mine on **CLEMSON*** rather quickly and sent it over to Clemson on Tuesday before the game. They ran it in their paper early in the week. They also were nice enough to make copies of the story and fax it to radio stations all over the state.

> …I just asked, "What excellence?" Clemson had a losing record against every SEC team except Vanderbilt.

When they did that, phone calls started pouring in. I got a call from my father on Wednesday morning in my dorm room in Athens. He said, "What in the world have you done?" I said, "What are you talking about?" He said, "This is all over the radio over here. I'm getting nasty phone calls

*When **CLEMSON** University plays in a bowl game, most of their fans pay their hotel and restaurant tabs with $2 bills to show their economic impact…and increase their chances of a future invitation.

19

at the house. What's going on?" I told him about the article I had written. The article commented on Clemson's so-called tradition of excellence. I just asked, "What excellence?" Clemson had a losing record against every SEC team except Vanderbilt. I'm a little embarrassed to say that, to this day, you can call the article up on Google, and it will pop up as the top option. The situation turned ugly. I got a lot of threats in my dorm room. There are friends of my parents who have not spoken to me since then, and these are people I grew up with. They took it very personally, and they were not supposed to. This was supposed to be our student newspaper and their student newspaper. This was not supposed to be radio fodder for the week, but it turned out to be. Fortunately, Georgia won the ball game.

As of about two or three years ago, that article was on the bulletin board in the Clemson Athletic Department, but I don't know if it still is. Some people saw the humor in it, but a lot of people didn't. What's funny is I also got a lot of calls from South Carolina fans thanking me for it, which was nice. A fellow called me from a bar in Greenwood, South Carolina, and told me that I could drink free for life in his bar whenever I come through town. I got a lot of mileage out of it, but it made people mad. But, you know, the truth makes people mad sometimes.

Night games are nice, and not just because of the extra tailgating time. There's something about the atmosphere of an early evening game in Athens that's really, really special. As stadiums go, Sanford ranks up there. I was a sportswriter for a number of years so I've been to most of the stadiums in this part of the country. It ranks up there with any of them in terms of game-day atmosphere. There are a few bad seats in the house, but every stadium has that. It's a heck of a facility.

Florida fans don't win well. I guess, at this point, they have every right to be that way. They clobber us every year it seems. That's going to have stop at some point. You can go to any other program—Tennessee, Auburn, Alabama—and generally speaking, people are going to get along. You see a lot of mixed crowds tailgating. You get your 'Bama fans and your Georgia fans—your Auburn fans and your Georgia fans! You don't see that at Georgia-Florida, where tailgating is completely separated, and probably for good reason. There's a lot of mouthing going on between those fan bases.

Florida fans tend to be different from the rest of the SEC. A lot of them are not from the South. You've got a lot of transplants from other parts of the country that have adopted Florida as their team. When Spurrier came along, they picked up a fan base that's probably not indicative of what that university has always been. It's not really a Southern school anymore. Florida's not a Southern state anymore and the fan base is indicative of that. Older Florida fans tend to be much, much easier to get along with than some of the ones who came along when they started winning 10 games a year under Spurrier. They remember. The older fans know that winning and losing go in cycles. A lot of Florida fans who have come along in the last 15 years think that Florida has always been winning football games, and that's simply not the case. That's one of the reasons that just about everybody in the SEC dislikes Florida. It's not so much the fact they're winning now—it's the fact they fail to recognize that they aren't the first to do it. Everybody in the upper tier of the SEC has had the type of roll they have been on. That's my theory anyway.

WE WON'T BE BACK RIGHT AFTER THIS

Wes Durham

Durham is 41 and lives in Atlanta. Since 1995, he's been the voice of the Georgia Tech Yellow Jackets in football and men's basketball. Since 2004, he's been the play-by-play announcer for the Atlanta Falcons. His father Woody Durham is the voice of North Carolina football and basketball.

I got to know Larry Munson in 1992 when I went to Vanderbilt to do their ball games. Larry had also spent time at Vanderbilt. Because my dad, Woody, is in the business, I've always had tremendous amounts of respect for guys who paved the way for today's college games on radio. Larry certainly falls into that classification.

Larry is a great resource. He's been a mentor to me. We get together and laugh and tell stories, but, at the same time, we also talk about the business and how the business is changing. He has always been a good friend, though we're probably not supposed to be very good friends, since we do rival's games. But, he's always been somebody I enjoy visiting with and somebody whose work I respect a great deal. When he retires, that'll be the end of his unique style. It will impossible for somebody to try to duplicate him at Georgia games. There may be points in a broadcasts where a different announcer could use a phrase he uttered at one point, but it won't be comfortable, and it won't be seamless, like it would have been had Larry done it.

> ...we're probably not supposed to be very good friends, since we do rival's games.

The biggest blessing I've had in this business is—you've heard the story—"My heroes have become my friends." Guys like Larry

Munson and Cawood Ledford and Jim Fife and Eli Gold and Jim Phillips, guys I grew up listening to when I was riding around with my dad, when he was doing ball games—and he still does them—it's neat.

Larry is easygoing outside the booth. We tend to be early arrivals to the Georgia-Georgia Tech game because we both hate traffic. We'll talk about music. He loves music and is a fairly accomplished piano player. He played with Sinatra or an Artie Shaw or somebody like that one time. He also loves movies. He can recall movies of years gone by. He's as good with actors and actresses in movies as anybody I've ever been around. He enjoys his life. He's obviously very pleased with what he's done, legacy-wise. At the same time, his boys are important to him. It might surprise people who think he's out to be the life of the party to hear that he is easygoing.

Like any good college football rivalry, the Georgia-**GEORGIA TECH*** rivalry is about history. The rivalry ties generations of families, as you can see by the 'house divided' license plates all over the state. The game, always held on Thanksgiving or the Saturday after, does not get the publicity or the notoriety that Auburn-Alabama get. Or that Florida-Florida State get. Or that Ohio State-Michigan get. Or Oregon-Oregon State at times. But it is just as important a rivalry as any of those, more so for Tech fans because they haven't been successful, particularly in the last 35 years.

*When TECH coach Chan Gailey played Little League baseball in his hometown of Americus, Georgia, his coach was Dan Reeves. Reeves, the former Falcons coach, was also from Americus.

HEAR ME NOW—LISTEN TO ME LATER

What I like best about Larry Munson is he's untarnished. He is a not-apologizing Georgia fan. To him, it's us against them. When he says, "Hunker down, you guys." He's saying what 60,000 people are saying in their minds. He takes the real special times and puts a voice to it. The rest of our lives we are listening to his broadcasts on our MP3s or CDs at our tailgates. It puts us all back in the action, the way he paints a picture. When he said about Herschel Walker, "He just ran over people. My God, a freshman." How many people, that year, said, "My God, a freshman," when they were talking about Herschel Walker.

The funny thing is when I hear him say that stuff, I see papers flying. I see people jumping up and down. I see him screaming. I see folks who weren't quite paying attention to the play suddenly paying attention because Larry is jumping up and down screaming. Then, out of the blue, he said, "I broke my chair."

—DR. WILLIAM BECK, Dentist, 52, Lawrenceville, Georgia

When Georgia plays on the road, I listen to Larry Munson call the games. He was one of the biggest parts of my childhood. My brother and I used to get up early on Saturday mornings to listen to him. My father has this old beat-up copy of a VHS tape called "25 Years of Georgia Football," that Warren Smith put together for Vince Dooley a couple of years after he retired. All these famous Larry Munson calls are on it. That was the first place we got exposed to him. I'm one of those people who will mute the television and put Larry Munson on the radio. I bring my headphones into the game. Part of going to the game is getting in the car afterward and listening to the post-game show on the radio.

—DAVID POLLACK, 27, Stone Mountain, Georgia

I've met Larry Munson any number of times. Where I'd usually cross paths with him is in the grocery store when he ran out of cigars. I find it very interesting that Mr. Munson has this movie group, principally girls. Bear in mind, he's in his eighties. He and a group of girls go to the movies together, then they rate them.

Sometimes on his program, "Larry Munson—Insight on Sports," he talks about the movies and the girls, instead of sports.

—LEN DAVIS, 63, Athens, Georgia

Growing up, we heard a lot of Larry Munson calls. You can't think about Georgia football without some of Larry's best calls. I was playing in the Tennessee, "hob-nail boot game." As soon as it was over, the media were asking us about the hob-nail boot. We had no idea what they were talking about. That's what Georgia football is—a series of Larry Munson quotes. Often when you run into people away from the set who work in radio or TV, it's like you're talking to a completely different person. But, with Larry, what you hear on the radio—that's him, the whole time, which I love. It's almost like a commentary when you talk to him. I think it's ingrained in him.

—JON STINCHCOMB, ex-Bulldog now with the New Orleans Saints

Larry Munson started in '66 when I was there. You think he's sitting in the booth breathing fire and drinking blood out of a cup, but he's a very gentle, easygoing guy. We traveled together to the Ole Miss game last year. We got back in Atlanta after a night

He has rendered beloved service to the university.

game around two-thirty or three in the morning. When you're 83 years old, that takes its toll. I can see why the away games are problematic for him. But, my problem with him is if I hear him on the radio doing a commercial for something my pulse rate goes up 25 points just because I hear that voice. He came on board as Georgia football really exploded. Our '66 and '68 teams won the conference. He was just getting started, and then they won the national championship in '80; so he's had some great years to do what he does. He has rendered beloved service to the university.

—DR. TOMMY LAWHORNE, Georgia linebacker '65-'68

When I was working with *The Red & Black*, there was one divorced guy with us named O.P. I'd known him a long time. He was a friend of our family, in his mid-forties. He was always the leader of the party crowd of my parents group. He didn't have a ticket for the Florida game, so I gave him my extra pass to the press box. We got into the Bloody Marys pretty good on the bus ride to the game and I had to give him a little lesson on press box etiquette when we arrived. I told him, "We don't show emotion in the press box. We're there just watching a game. You're not a fan. You have to make some effort to look like you're a working press and sit to the side—no cheering." He was pretty well behaved during the first quarter.

> Munson's screams of joy turned to, "That dastardly flag. That hanky—NO."

Unbeknownst to me, he had slipped a flask of bourbon in his sock. During the second quarter, the bourbon came out as the Cokes came around. I said, "O.P., you can't be drinking in the press box." The game went on. Halftime came and went. The game got exciting. I slipped my Coke to him and said, "All right, just tip that flask in my cup here for a second." By the fourth quarter, Georgia was on the verge of upsetting the #6 ranked Florida Gators. Fueled by a little bit of the flask contents, I was the one who, in the middle of the fourth quarter, screamed out in the press box, breaking all the etiquette rules, "Let's go Dawgs! Come on." O.P. grabbed me and said, "I thought we had to behave in here. I thought there was no cheering." As it happened, the whole press box got caught up in the game, and all those grizzled guys turned into fans one way or the other. It was a tremendous finish. I hung out the press box screaming and yelling right along with Munson—the fan—two seats down from me.

Georgia had this momentum-changing play at that Georgia-Florida game by our big running back, Glynn Harrison. He broke the line, got to the sideline and ran down the right side in front of us. With that run, I erupted. I was watching Larry two seats down from me. He was screaming, describing the run by Harrison that was going to break for a touchdown. Ten-fifteen yards from him scoring, a flag went down at mid-field. There had been a clip on the play. Munson's screams of joy turned to, "That dastardly flag. That hanky—NO." He cursed the appearance of the flag that indicated clipping on Georgia. His emotion went from genuine excitement, "we have finally gotten the play that is going to get us in this game and make us competitive," to the depths of depression.

Munson screamed at that yellow flag. "That dastardly flag. That awful, terrible color is on the green grass now—that yellow flag is going to wipe this play out, and we're right back to where we began, and we've got no hope at all again, and it's all because of that dastardly flag. That yellow color on the green grass has just dashed Georgia's hopes." We all sat back down. The flag just took the air out of that stadium. The stadium went from shaking one minute on the Georgia side, while Harrison was in the midst of the run, to deathly quiet the next minute. I've never seen such a swing of emotion. Munson captured it perfectly.

> ... in Munson's voice, you hear the heartbreak that the Georgia fans were feeling at that moment.

It's easy to be the home-team announcer when the game is going great. But, nobody portrays the suffering of the crowd over the microphone like Munson does when things have gone wrong on the field. It's one thing to describe the other team making a big play and they scored on you. But, in Munson's voice, you hear the heartbreak that the Georgia fans were feeling at that moment. He relays it better than anybody I've ever heard. That's what draws everybody to him. The Georgia fans know that Munson is one of them.

—RICK FRANZMAN, 55, former sports editor of *The Red & Black*

Larry Munson is a "homer." He's a true Bulldog in every sense of the word. He gets so excited. Before the game, everything he says is pessimistic. "We don't have a chance." "The whole line is 20 pounds bigger than us." "They're faster than us." "They've got so much team speed." "All of those seniors, and we're playing our freshmen!" He just goes on and on and on. I love it. I don't know what we're going to do when he's not there.

—MERCER CROOK, 60, Gainesville, Georgia

There was a big article in the paper recently about Larry Munson. There's word going around he had a meeting with Damon Evans, the athletic director. Munson's 85, and he's not in good health. He's at the age where he's missing some things. Heck, I'm 77. I make mistakes.

Larry's got a lot of great lines. Back in 1980 at the Florida game, Florida was ahead with a little over a minute to go. Buck Belue was the Georgia quarterback, and we were on our 8-yard line, second down. Belue threw a pass about 25 yards up the left side to Lindsay Scott, who was wide open. He caught the ball and ran for a touchdown to beat Florida. This was before the remodeling on the Gator Bowl. Munson said, "Well, the stadium's gonna collapse now." Then he talked about condos up in St. Simons, "There's going to be some property destroyed tonight." In my lifetime, that was probably the greatest description of one play.

> Munson said, "Well, the stadium's gonna collapse now."

Larry will go down in history as one of the great broadcasters of football. He's a born pessimist. A lot of people don't like that. Georgia is never going to have a good football team at the start of the season, as far as he's concerned. He's always worried about injuries. He's always concerned about somebody not being eligible and we're going to lose this, and we're going to lose that. He's had a great career at Georgia.

Larry is a lifetime member of the Touchdown Club. He's talked to us a couple or three times. He's not a great speaker. If you talk to him, it would be a tough interview for you, but he's just that way. The cheerleaders have a little party at his house every year on Friday night before the first game. I've been going for the last three years. Last year, he came out in his pajamas and made about a two-minute talk. Then he went back in the house and sat down in his living room. If you wanted to speak to him, you had to get in line.

—CANDLER MEADORS, 78, Atlanta native, Athens car dealer

I remember Joe Eaves, our athletic director called me into his office in the late summer of 1966. I was sports information director and we had just lost Ed Thilenius, a very good announcer, who had gone with a TV station in Atlanta. He was doing the Atlanta Braves baseball games, too. Coach Eaves asked me what I thought of Larry Munson succeeding Ed Thilenius. I said, "Well, I've never heard him call a football game. I've heard him call the Vanderbilt basketball games." He was in Nashville, Tennessee at that time and was very good calling the basketball games. Coach Eaves said,

"You can announce to the news media tomorrow that he's going to replace Ed Thilenius as our play-by-play man." That was in 1966, and he's still doing it. He's in his eighties now. He's not in the best of health. Larry Munson has been a fabulous play-by-play football announcer.

When we were on road trips, every night before the game, he and I and the sports writers would go out. We'd have a few beers, of course. I haven't made the road trips lately, and haven't seen much of him. I am in the press box for every home game and I go by the radio booth and say hello.

—DAN MAGILL, 87, former sports information director

I have been a Bulldog fan ever since I can remember. We didn't go to a lot of games when I was a kid, but we went to a few back in the old Sanford Stadium before they bowled in the end, when the railroad tracks were there. We could sit on the railroad tracks. I've been a fan of Larry Munson and, in fact, I always carry my portable radio and listen to him broadcast the game.

> We can be winning by 42 points, and Larry says, "Well, they've got a chance to come back. We've got to keep them down."

If it's an away game, I tune in to WSB or whoever is carrying the game on TV, and turn the sound down, and I listen to him broadcast the game.

We can be winning by 42 points, and Larry says, "Well, they've got a chance to come back. We've got to keep them down." He has that pessimistic outlook. He keeps us in check, so we don't get too cocky. Vince Dooley was like that, too. We could be playing Vanderbilt and be favored by 60 points, and he'd come out in the press, "You know, Vanderbilt's a tough team. We've got to be on our toes. These guys could jump up and surprise us." I've been hearing that ever since I've listened to Georgia football. Larry is a classic. I'm going to really hate it when he gives it up for good.

—JAY ABBOTT, Douglasville, Georgia

In 1999, my old friend, Travis Rice, was working for the local TV station, the cable-access station that bought up large blocks of time on cable access, and they were doing local commercial TV on cable access and they were always looking for programming. Travis and I went to games together and sat around sports bars and talked about sports. Eventually, we started going to a sports bar and taking a camera with us. We would sit and talk every week—the same conversation we would have been having in one of our living rooms. We just were having it in front of a camera, and we did it as a **TV SHOW*** from 1999 to 2004. We called it *The Dawg Show*. It was during football season, 30 minutes every week, we sat around and talked about football. We would do different segments. We would do a segment where we would pick the upcoming week's games. There was a segment I did called "too much information," which was statistical, historical background on this week's opponent. Because it was a 30-minute show, 22 minutes of actual air time, I'd prepare a lot of material that just wasn't really able to fit on the TV show. I didn't want it to go to waste so I got to where I would send out emails to people…"Here's some stuff I came up with for this week's show that didn't make it on." It started to getting to where people would forward it to other people. I was probably sending it to 100-odd people. One of them was Paul Westerdawg, who does a Georgia sports blog called georgiasports.blogspot.com. He wrote me one time and said, "You need to start a web blog with this instead of just sending it out as an email." Eventually, I wound up doing just that.

—T. KYLE KING, 38, Jonesboro, GA

I like to watch the game on the radio. The picture is better.
—STAN TORGERSON, long-time Ole Miss radio voice

---

*The first coach with his own **TV SHOW** was Bud Wilkinson at the University of Oklahoma in 1952.

Chapter 2

Growing Up A Bulldog

12 Years Old Forever

IF IT LOOKS LIKE A DUCKY
IF IT TALKS LIKE A DUCKY
IT'S DUCKY WALL—WORLD FAMOUS
ALL OVER ALBANY, GEORGIA

Ducky Wall

Ducky Wall was the long-time Sports Director for WALB-TV in Albany. He now works for the Physical Education Department at Darton College in Albany, Georgia.

Tech fans are tough, but there are not many of them. For the Georgia-Georgia Tech game a lot of Georgia fans will buy Georgia Tech season tickets just so they can get that one ticket to see Georgia play. Tech's stadium only seats about 45,000 fans. They made that stadium smaller—it used to seat about 59,000. Now they're trying to enlarge it again. Georgia's stadium seats 93,000, so when Tech fans come to Athens, they look like a little tiny blip in the corner of the end zone.

I remember picnicking with my mother and daddy. I know this will sound strange, but there's a graveyard on the other side of the railroad tracks right by Sanford Stadium in Athens. Dad used to always park in the cemetery because they had big shade trees. We'd picnic there and then we'd walk across the railroad tracks into the stadium. I can close my eyes and still see Mother and Daddy, who passed away years ago, and me and my brother walking in together, and my heart beats as fast as it does when the Bulldogs come out to warm up.

> Dad used to always park in the cemetery because they had big shade trees.

I was in television when Pat Dye became the head coach at Auburn. The first player

Pat Dye signed to Auburn was an offensive lineman from Albany. I told Pat, "Here we meet again in this boy's living room. I haven't seen you in about ten years, and you're signing your first athlete." We left there and went to Tifton, and Pat signed his second player. I taped both and did interviews with him about why he picked those boys.

Back in the '70s, we could go down on the sideline before the game. I remember in 1976, I stood right by Bear Bryant while he was watching his team warm up under the goalpost. I didn't say anything to him, and he didn't say anything to me.

When Vince Dooley retired, Ray Goff became Georgia's head coach. Ray and I were real good friends. He wanted to have a party for all the high school coaches in southwest Georgia. My backyard is about two acres, so we decided to have it there. That party continued through the Goff and Donnan years and then through Mark Richt's first two years.

> "Vince, you've given all the south Georgia players to the north coach."

Ray played quarterback in Moultrie, Georgia, which is about 40 miles from Albany. I was in my glory back then with the fans of southwest Georgia. For some strange reason, they thought Ducky hung the moon. When Ray was in high school, we covered them. They won a state championship with him as quarterback. We were always right there with the cameras. Ray knew me long before he went on to star as a quarterback at Georgia and become head coach there. I really enjoyed those years.

Georgia had what they called the G-Day game in the spring. In 1980, Vince Dooley was head coach, and he invited me up to be one of the coaches for the red and black game. When I saw the roster, I said, "Vince, you've given all the south Georgia players to the north coach. I don't have any. I've got boys I don't even know." We had a great day. They had a big feed for us before the game. I met all the players. They gave me a brand new Georgia shirt. I thought I'd died and gone to heaven with that on. My team got their butts beat 30-17, but we still had fun. Georgia won the national championship that fall, and, of course, I take full credit for training all those boys (which is a lie, but it was fun). That was a big day in my life. They gave me a beautiful plaque, which still hangs on my wall in our family room.

Does your Alma Matter?

SOUTH OF CHATTANOOGA, THE SIGN SAYS WELCOME TO GEORGIA. IT DOESN'T SAY A DAMN THING ABOUT GEORGIA TECH

Dewey Moody

Dewey Moody, 59, is a UGA grad and an employee of Alcoa in Norcross, Georgia. He is also State Communications Director of the Full Gospel Business Men's Fellowship International. He and his wife Brenda live in Grayson, Georgia.

What I like most about the Georgia-Georgia Tech game is winning. I take it pretty hard when we lose to Tech. If we go 1-10, I can live with that, as long as that one win is against Tech.

The worst thing I remember happening at that game was when we got a fumble called against us inside the one-yard line. Tech ended up winning that game in overtime. The officials later admitted they had blown the call. Ever since then, I've really been bitter toward Tech.

I started school at Georgia in '67. I didn't start my season tickets until I graduated in '71. I've only missed one home game since 1967, and that was last fall when my wife was critically ill. She's doing better now. My freshman year was the first year they added the upper decks on each side. We take a lot of pride in the stadium at Georgia. I have seen it in all the phases from the upper deck on each side to the closing of the end zone and the closing of the opposite end zone up to the 93,000 it seats now. I have a lot of fond memories of the stadium and all the home games through the years.

We go to all the away games. The nicest fans we meet are at Ole Miss. They still have Southern hospitality there. They speak to you. They ask you if you need anything. They welcome you to their campus. It is a friendly, nice place to visit. Their theme is "where the old South still lives."

I've been to all the stadiums in the SEC. South Carolina is a pretty intense rivalry now. Their fans are probably the most obnoxious of anywhere we go. They hate Georgia so. Spurrier hates Georgia. South Carolina joined the SEC late, but Georgia played them many times when they were in the ACC. So the Georgia-South Carolina rivalry was already there when South Carolina left the ACC and came into the SEC.

Herschel Scott, Mr. Bulldog, is considered the greatest Georgia fan who ever lived. He died three years ago, in his eighties. He had little business cards made up. He had not missed a Georgia home, away or bowl game since the 1950s. For the last 15 years of his life, he was widowed, and he rode with my wife and me to the out-of-town games. He was the one who said he hated Tech so bad he wouldn't even eat mustard on his hot dog cause he hated the color yellow! He was a character. He knew all the Georgia coaches back to Wally Butts.

> "Bulldog born, Bulldog bred, here I lie, Bulldog dead."

On his granite tombstone is a big Bulldog head. On his wife's side is a line from the Edgar Allan Poe poem "Annabelle Lee," "She was loved with a love that was more than love." On his side is his name and the words, **"Bulldog born, Bulldog bred, here I lie, Bulldog dead."** He had it all fixed before he died—across the bottom, it said "blank consecutive Georgia games." I think they filled it in with 480-something that he had seen without missing one.

We are tremendously blessed to have Mark Richt as our coach. I wouldn't trade him for anybody in the nation. As far as recruiting, coaching and integrity, there is nobody I rank higher than Mark Richt. He is a remarkable Christian man.

Georgia football has been the greatest hobby of my life. I have a slight disability from having polio as a child. I've never been real active as far as golf or tennis or hunting or fishing, so the Bulldogs have been my #1 hobby. They've brought me many happy hours and years.

When Joe Paterno takes his glasses off, does his nose come off, too?

HEY, DID YOU KNOW THAT AUBURN'S A FOUR-YEAR SCHOOL NOW?

Mark King

King grew up in Dalton, Georgia, in a family of Georgia Tech and Auburn fans. He finally set the family on the right track by choosing Georgia, where he graduated in 1982. He has lived in Fresno, California, for the past 19 years.

When I moved to Fresno, people told me that Fresno was a football town, so, I bought season tickets to the Fresno State football games. The first time I went, I was stunned. The stadium was half empty until mid-way through the second quarter. I said, "Where is everybody?" They said, "We've got to have our parties." I explained how it is at Georgia. The parties start Wednesday night. By Saturday, you're ready to dry out a little bit, and it's time for football. When it's kickoff time at a Georgia game on Saturday, everybody's inside the stadium. So not only are people here in Fresno late, but they also sit down while the game is playing. I tried to explain that at Georgia, and a lot of the other SEC schools, unless you're in the luxury skyboxes, while the game is going on, you stand up. You might sit down during halftime or during the TV timeouts. During the actual action, you're on your feet. It's important.

With all due respect to everyone else, there's nothing like Southeastern Conference football. I have no problem with the people out here who root for Fresno State. Every once in a while, somebody will learn that I'm a Georgia graduate. They'll say, "Oh, the other Bulldogs." And, I'll say, "You mean the 1942 and 1980 national champion Bulldogs?" Then, they want to change the subject. I don't know why. All of a sudden, they want to talk about something else. "No, we're not the other Bulldogs—we're THE Bulldogs!"

I grew up in Dalton, up in the northwest corner of the state, in a family where people either went to Auburn or Georgia Tech. Those were the two big schools in my family. You have to understand about Southern football sentiments—it was very, very difficult for me to imagine going to the University of Georgia when I was a teenager. Auburn people and Georgia Tech people, especially, tend not to care for the University of Georgia. I grew up not being a Georgia fan. In fact, the opposite—I would root against Georgia.

Most people in my family are engineers. I just presumed that's what I was going to be as I was growing up. Then, in the eleventh grade in high school, I took this class called analysis of trigonometry. I could do it, but it was agony for me. I said, "I don't want to go to engineering school. I was going to go to the University of Tennessee, simply to avoid going to the University of

> My heart darn near leaps out of my chest every time I'm in Athens.

Georgia. Then, one day, I saw the light and chose Georgia! I'm so glad I went to the University of Georgia. I had a blast. My heart darn near leaps out of my chest every time I'm in Athens. It's a magical place for me, and it always will be.

Every time I've been back to the stadium, I go to the mausoleum where the Ugas are buried. I have my wife or my son take a picture of me putting flowers by the mausoleum. They've both asked me, "Do we have to get some flowers?" "Hey, don't worry about it. There'll be plenty of flowers there." And, there always are. So, I just pick some up and make it look like I did it. It's a nice little picture of me laying flowers at Uga's tomb.

Mark Richt is a gentleman and a classy guy. That's important to Georgia. To have people associate me, simply because I'm a graduate of the school, with such a wonderful and successful program is exciting. A lot of places I go in California, people will notice my University of Georgia ring and they'll comment about the Bulldogs. Anybody who knows me knows I'm a University of Georgia graduate. I've got Georgia paraphernalia in my office. I've got it in my home. I wear my Georgia ring, which I'm very proud of, every day. We've got a group here in Fresno who get together every Saturday in the fall to watch the Georgia games together. It's funny, only two of us in the group grew up in Georgia. All the other people grew up in some other state and went to school at Georgia, but they got infected with the same fever while they were there, even though they're not Southerners. To be with this group every Saturday in the fall and watch the games, although not as exciting as being in the stadium, is very special and in some ways it brings me back to Athens and my college days. Even my wife has been infected. She's a California girl, but she has Georgia clothes she wears to the football-watching parties. She's excited to be associated with the University of Georgia. All of her friends know that she's a Georgia fan. It's a wonderful thing to be associated with.

> The single thing that I miss the most about the Deep South is being able to talk college football...

I don't plan on leaving California. I like it a lot. The single thing that I miss the most about the Deep South is being able to talk college football with somebody any day of the year.

DEEP THOUGHTS, CHEAP SHOTS AND BON MOTS

Living in Athens as I child, we got to play football at the YMCA. I started playing in the fourth grade, and we played at a high level. By the time I was in the sixth grade, we would play against the high school B teams. We could beat most of the B teams around, even though a lot of the guys on our team were only in the sixth grade. Before the Georgia games, the "Y" would play three or four games on the football field starting at about eleven o'clock in the morning. They'd divide the football field up and instead of playing lengthwise, we'd play sideline to sideline, so they'd have about three games going on at a time. Afterward, we'd get to sit in the end zone and watch the games and see the big guys up close when they'd come on and off the field. That was a real thrill as a kid.

—JIM MASSEY, 60, retired, grew up in Athens

Growing up, I was probably the only kid in my elementary school that was a Bulldog fan. Everybody else was a Georgia Tech fan. All the other boys wore Georgia Tech rat hats to school every day—those little beanies the freshmen at Tech used to wear. This was back when Bobby Dodd was coaching at Georgia Tech and they were winning championships. Georgia didn't have very good teams back then.

I listened to Ed Thilenius on the radio. He could keep me interested in the game. His nickname was the "Gentleman Sportscaster". He was very high-toned, very dramatic. Larry Munson is intense. Ed Thilenius was dramatic. He called the games in the late fifties to early sixties. Munson took his place.

Ed Thelinius always said, "Imagine the radio is your field," which just set the tone for a kid sitting in front of a radio listening to a football game. "Imagine the radio is your field, the Bulldogs are moving left to right. Clemson is moving..." That kind of thing. He could really set the stage for the game. Listening to him was like attending a play or an opera.

—GREG GRIFFIN, 59, attorney, Marietta, Georgia

Recently, I had to drive to the other side of Atlanta to pick up a Methodist minister from North Carolina, Dr. Darrel Starnes. He was going to spend the night at our home and preach at our church the next morning. When I picked him up, he looked at the back of my truck and saw my Georgia sticker. He made some comment about Georgia and told me that he had grown up in Knoxville and was a Tennessee fan. When I got him to my home, I took him down into my basement, which is decorated all in red and black. There's a Georgia light over the pool table. Everything in the room is Georgia. I tried to show him the error of his ways and convert him. The next morning in church, he got up and was talking about my wife's cooking. Then, he went on to talk about never having seen so much red and black and all about the Tennessee Vols, and what not. After the service, I went up to him and said, "Well, I must have done some good. You have on a black robe with red trim." He said, "Oh, those are God's colors." I said, "That's what I've been trying to tell you."

—STEVE STANCIL, 55, Canton, Georgia

Chapter 3

Sweet Home Sanford

The Field of Screams
in the Land of Ahs

CIGAREETS AND WHUSKEY AND WILD, WILD WOMEN

Rick Franzman

Franzman, 55, lives in Marietta. He is a furniture manufacturers representative. Franzman was the sports editor and executive editor of The Red & Black. *He graduated from the University of Georgia in '75.*

O ne of the unique things about Georgia football back when I was there was the train track on the east side of the stadium. We used to have 5,000 people on that hill to watch the game. It was as good as a lot of the end zone seats in modern stadiums. That was a raucous crowd. The cool thing about sitting up there for a Saturday afternoon game was that we would have to get there at nine o'clock in the morning to stake out a seat. Everybody would bring their coolers. The party would actually start the Friday night before and would roll right into that Saturday morning. The team buses would show up at about eleven o'clock in the morning on the street below the hill. When the buses roared up with sirens blasting, those 5,000 people on the hill sounded like the whole stadium. They'd stand up as the players came off the buses, and the players would always salute us die-hards. The dark side of that story is the cemetery on the other side of the train track. That's where everybody had to go when nature called. That crowd up there was wild.

> But one guy volunteered to go if somebody would loan him a car. I had never seen the guy before.

At times, a train would actually come through. That was always a funny sight. Everybody would have to get up and move off the tracks. More than one or two inebriated people would be falling all over themselves trying to get off the train tracks as the train moved through at five miles an hour. Well down the tracks, it would start blowing its horn as a signal for everybody in the stadium to turn and watch thousands of people get up and move their positions and their coolers around. The train came through about every other game and the conductor waved to the crowd.

I was sitting on the train tracks one Saturday afternoon. We had exhausted our fuel supply. It was only halftime, and we didn't know how we were going to make it through the rest of the game. We'd been begging, borrowing and stealing booze from everybody around us. The group I was with finally decided we needed to refuel. But, the idea of leaving the tracks, getting a car, going to the liquor store, buying more beer and liquor and then trying to find parking on campus was absurd. But one

> I'd figured out how to get rid of kudzu—turn 5,000 UGA students with beer loose on it for four months.

guy volunteered to go if somebody would loan him a car. I had never seen the guy before. In a moment of clouded judgment, I handed him the keys to my car, told him where it was parked and what it looked like. We gave him money and told him to get us beer. He left and that was the last we saw of him. After the game, we realized what happened. I sobered up fast and faced the fact that I just let somebody drive off with my car. I was distraught. My buddies kept saying, "What kind of an idiot are you? You gave the guy your car." I said, "Well, it seemed like a good idea at the time." We were walking around and I was just about ready to go to the police and report the car stolen when, by absolute chance, I stumbled across my car. It was in the middle of a back parking lot, hundreds of yards from where it had been originally parked. Most of the crowd had cleared out, and there was my car, unlocked with the keys in it. We five guys hopped in and headed off to celebrate another Bulldog victory!

The hill with the train tracks used to be covered with kudzu, a nasty ivy-like vine that southerners imported from Japan as a ground cover back during the depression. Kudzu takes over at the beginning in the spring and it's impossible to get rid of all summer and fall. At the beginning of the football season, it covered the hill from top to bottom. It became an engineering project to figure out how to get rid of it. Nobody could figure it out. By the end of football season, the hill would be bare. There'd be no kudzu left on it. I used to write in my column that I'd figured out how to get rid of kudzu—turn 5,000 UGA students with beer loose on it for four months. There would be no kudzu left.

In 1968, Georgia beat Florida 51-0. Florida was lucky to score 0.

OUTSIDE OF A DOG, A BOOK IS MAN'S BEST FRIEND. INSIDE OF A DOG, IT'S TOO DARK TO READ.

Frank "Sonny" Seiler

Seiler, 75, is the owner of the late great Uga VI and his five predecessors. He graduated from UGA law school in 1957 and is a senior partner at Bouhan Williams & Levy LLP, the Savannah law firm featured in Midnight in the Garden of Good and Evil.

We got the bulldog in April 1956, when he was a puppy. He did not look anything like the Georgia mascot or even a bulldog for that matter. He was skinny and gangly like all bulldog puppies start out. By September, he had grown and had his shoulders and looked like the hood ornament on a Mack truck. At the time, Georgia did not have a mascot because Mike, a bulldog, had died after serving as mascot in the early 1950s.

We were not thinking mascot when we dressed him up in a red tee shirt that my wife had made from a child's tee shirt. She fashioned a black felt "G" and stitched it on the chest. She put elastic around the cuffs and the waist. We took him over to the Sigma Chi fraternity house before the game just for fun, not planning to take him to the game. After several iced teas, everybody said, "Let's take him to the game. Let's take him to the game." All we had to do was walk across the street to the stadium, so we took him to the game—not on the field, mind you, but up in the stands. In those days they let real bulldogs into the stands. He got a lot of attention.

Some Associated Press photographer took pictures of him, which ended up in *The Atlanta Constitution.* Dan Magill, our tennis coach, who was then the athletic publicity director, told Coach Butts, "Sonny Seiler has a white English bulldog puppy that would make us a good mascot. Why don't you see if he'll let us use him?"

> "Sonny, Dan tells me you've got an English bulldog puppy that might make us a good mascot...."

I worked in the ticket office during law school. When I went to work on Tuesday after the game, there was a note from my boss that Coach Butts wanted to see me in his office. I went up, hat in hand, wondering what the hell I had done and hoping I wasn't about to be fired because I really needed the job. He said, "Sonny, Dan tells me you've got an English bulldog puppy that might make us a good mascot. What do you say about letting us use him to create some excitement? I don't seem to be making any." He laughed, because we weren't very good. What was I going to say to the big boss? "Of course." That's how it all started.

We took him to all the games, and he caught on. But, the next year, I had to tell Coach Butts, "I don't want to be an Indian giver, but I'm graduating and I've got to go in the Army. I'll be around Savannah and I promise you we'll have the dog at every game, but I'd like to keep him with me." He said, "Sounds like a good deal to me, Sonny."...

Attending the Heisman Trophy banquet in 1982 was a fabulous experience. We flew Uga to New York on the same plane with Herschel Walker and his family. We stayed at the Hilton Hotel and took him to the banquet. This was not when it was announced that Herschel had won, this was the big banquet that was later in December.

How can any bowl game get any better than winning the national championship? People think it's great to be on the sidelines, and I've been there all my life. I've probably seen more Georgia games from the sidelines than any living man. It's not a good place to watch football though. First of all, when you have the dog, you've got to be aware of the animal at all times, of safety, of sidelines rules and all that. Although my son actually holds Uga, I am usually there. Second, you can't see the game very well. You lose depth perception from the 30-yard line in. I'm used to it because I've been down there for so long. I just try to stay out of the way.

The April 27, 1997, cover of **_SPORTS ILLUSTRATED_*** featured Uga V for an article on **_America's Top 50 Jock Schools,_** with a caption **_"No. 1 Mascot, Uga V."_** I didn't know anything about Uga being on the cover of *Sports Illustrated* until a friend called me and asked me if I'd seen the magazine. I didn't even subscribe. I told him I hadn't seen it, and he said, "Well, you'd better get it because Uga V's on the cover, and they've named him the most outstanding college mascot in the country." I immediately set out to get a copy. The dogs had been in *Sports Illustrated* many times, but never on the cover. They had sent a photographer to Savannah several weeks before to take a new round of pictures, but I didn't know, nor did he that Uga was going to be picked for the cover....

> "...because Uga V's on the cover, and they've named him the most outstanding college mascot in the country."

I represented Jim Williams, who was the defendant in the real life murder trial in Savannah depicted in the book and movie, *Midnight in the Garden of Good and Evil.* I also knew John Berendt, the author, because I worked with him when he wrote the book. Clint Eastwood, who directed the movie, came to Savannah on a Saturday and wanted to see Uga while he was here. He fell in love

---

*In 1955, _SPORTS ILLUSTRATED_ selected horse owner William Woodward as their Sportsman of the Year. Woodward's wife shot and killed the unfaithful Woodward before the issue went to press. S.I. then selected World Series hero, Johnny Podres.

with the dog. He got down on the floor and was wrestling with him. Then, Mr. Eastwood looked up at my wife and said to the dog, "Uga, I'm going to make you a celebrity." Cecelia said, "With all due respect Mr. Eastwood, Uga's already a celebrity."...

A ceremony in the stadium October 22, 1966 retired Uga I and introduced Uga II. The crowd responded with an impromptu "Damn Good Dawg" chant, something we never expected! We knew the dog was appreciated and well liked, but we didn't know that he had caught on as well as he had with the fans and the students. It was a pleasant surprise for him to get that kind of sendoff, and for the new dog to get that kind of welcome.

> " Mr. Eastwood, Uga's already a celebrity. " ...

It was exciting for Uga and for us to be chauffeured to the Auburn game by my Auburn friend, Jack Swertfeger. It was a strange sight to see a real devoted War Eagle like Jack dressed in orange and blue from head to toe driving a car with the Georgia mascot, wearing his uniform, and all the rest of us wearing red and black. It surprised the police, who were stationed at key intersections, more than anybody. At one stop they thought the dog had been stolen and was being carted off by some wild Auburn fan. But Jack helped us with the police. I wish we could go back and relive some of those days.

At another event, Steve Spurrier was lined up with some others to parade into a banquet hall. Spurrier got out of line and came over to pat Uga on the head. It was a touching scene. We exchanged a few pleasant words, and he got back in the line. Of course, that was before he went to Florida as a coach and beat the hell out of us for so long. My feelings for him are still the same. I think he's a great football coach and obviously a nice human being to take time to pay respects to an opponent's mascot.

My association with the University of Georgia has been very exciting and very rewarding, and I wouldn't swap places with anybody in this world.

IN THE 4TH QUARTER OF HIS CAREER... PRAYIN' FOR OVERTIME

Dan Magill

Say the name Dan Magill to the Bulldog Nation and everyone smiles. The Living Legend, 87, joined Wally Butts in the Athletic Department in 1949, and he's still there as the curator of the College Men's Tennis Hall Of Fame. The World War II Marine originated the Georgia Bulldog Clubs in every county in the state. The tennis complex bears his name.

I was born in Athens, Georgia, January 25, 1921. I grew up on the Georgia athletic fields. I was **BATBOY*** and a foul-ball chaser with the baseball team in 1931, when I was 10 years old. I hung around the Georgia athletic campus all the time. The pitcher on the 1931 Georgia baseball team was a boy from nearby Collinsville, Georgia, named Spurgeon Chandler. He went on to be a great pitcher for the **NEW YORK YANKEES***. He was baseball's most valuable pitcher in 1943. He set a record of 20 wins and 4 losses. He was a star pitcher for the New York Yankees on four of their world championship teams. That's my earliest memory of being the batboy and foul-ball chaser.

> *As a young boy in Newcomerstown, Ohio, Woody Hayes was a <u>BATBOY</u> for a semi-pro baseball team managed by Cy Young.

> *<u>YANKEE</u> Stadium is known as "the House that Ruth Built." The school that Babe Ruth attended in his youth, St. Mary's Industrial School for Boys in Baltimore—now called Cardinal Gibbons High School—was known as "the House that Built Ruth." ...The cement used to build Yankee Stadium was purchased from Thomas Edison who owned the huge Portland Cement Company.

When I was a boy, I used to cut the grass in Sanford Stadium. I was a flunkie and hung around the athletic fields. I knew how to do everything in the athletic department. I eavesdropped on our great athletic director, Herman Stegeman every time he'd talk to a coach or to alumni. I could have coached every sport. Of course, I did play about every sport there was.

Coach Stegeman was my idol as a boy. He played at the **UNIVERSITY OF CHICAGO*** and was Amos Alonzo Stagg's greatest all-around athlete. He was a star lineman on the 1913 national championship team. He was just a great all-around athlete. He's the only coach Georgia ever had who coached four different sports—the major sports—football, baseball, basketball and track—to conference championships. He died of a heart attack in 1939 at the age of only 48. I was a sophomore then.

> He's the only coach Georgia ever had who coached four different sports...to conference championships.

I managed the tennis courts on campus during the summers when I was in high school and in college. Then I coached the young boys. I didn't know much about tennis, but I knew more than they did. I taught them how to play, but I gradually learned a great deal about tennis, too. You know, "on-the-job training". I was captain-elect of Georgia's team for the upcoming 1942 season, but World War II came along, and we didn't have a team. I later took up tennis and became a good senior player. I was the only player in the history of the Southern Senior Championship to play in every age division from 45 to 85. The main thing I learned was to clear the net. School's over if you knock the ball into the net.

The Georgia tennis complex is named after me. I've forgotten what year they named it, sometime in the 1990s, I guess. We have

---

*By winning percentage, Indiana ranks 12th in all-time Big Ten Football standings behind the **UNIVERSITY OF CHICAGO**.

the greatest **TENNIS*** layout of any college in the country. We have beautiful gardens and our stadium is the biggest of any college stadium. It seats over 4,000 fans, which is big. I don't coach this team, but one of my former stars, Manuel Diaz, of San Juan, Puerto Rico, does. Diaz was a great All-American player and then he became my assistant coach. He's done a fabulous job as head coach of the team. He's had three teams that have won the NCAA tournament, 1991, 2001 and 2007. He's had about six teams that were runner-up.

> To go from a tag-along kid to having a big athletic complex named after me was very rewarding.

To go from a tag-along kid to having a big athletic complex named after me was very rewarding. It makes me feel humble. I still come to work every morning here at the Hall of Fame. We have the greatest collection of tennis rackets of any museum in the world. We have the same model racket used by every national intercollegiate champion, singles and doubles, since the very first one, Joseph S. Clark of Harvard in 1883.

We've had so many great athletes at Georgia. Francis Tarkenton led us to the Southeastern Conference Championship against Auburn in a very famous game in 1959. It was fourth down and 13 yards to go. He hit the left end, Bill Herron, on fourth down for the touchdown pass. That tied the score at 13-13. Then Durwood Pennington kicked the extra point, and we won 14-13. That was one of the most thrilling football games in the history of Sanford Stadium. Francis Tarkenton went on to have a great 18-year career in the NFL, where he was an All-Pro player. He was a hometown boy.

*In 1974 Chris Evert was the leading money winner in which sport? TENNIS? Wrong! It was horse racing. A well-known trainer named his horses for tennis greats. His horse named Chris Evert was the leading money winner in 1974.

Herschel Walker was a wonderful young man from Wrightsville, Georgia. Herschel was big, about 215 pounds, which is big for a back, who was supposed to have been the fastest back in the country in that day. If you're 215 pounds and the fastest player, too, that's a lot of weight for speed to overcome.

My wife taught freshman English for 25 years at Georgia. She recalls this story about Herschel. It was the day before the big Florida game in Jacksonville. All the students like to take off a day or two in advance and spend the whole weekend down there. My wife had scheduled a big test for Friday, but the students all wanted to leave school Thursday and be gone for a long weekend. They asked her to please schedule the test another day. She said, "Well, all you students who are going to be gone this weekend, raise your hand. If you don't want to be here Friday, raise your hand." Every student but one raised his or her hand. The only student that didn't raise his hand was Herschel Walker. She said, "Herschel, they're going down to see you play." He said, "But we don't leave till Friday afternoon, by plane." He wasn't a great student, but he never missed a class, my wife said. He worked hard, and he passed. He had great character.

We've had so many championship football teams. Our **1942*** team went to the January 1, 1943 **ROSE BOWL***. Frank Sinkwich won the Heisman award that year. We used the single-wing formation, and he was the tailback. A sensational sophomore— freshmen weren't eligible then—Charley Trippi had made the team. Coach Butts moved Sinkwich to fullback late in the year and had Trippi at the tailback position. We won the Rose Bowl game against UCLA 9-0. Sinkwich scored the touchdown, but he had two sprained ankles and didn't play much in that game. Trippi was the star of the game. He's on the all-time Rose Bowl

*The Rose Bowl Parade originally had nothing to do with the Rose Bowl football game. It was a celebration in Pasadena for the ripening of the oranges....The 1942 ROSE BOWL game between Oregon State and Duke was played in Durham, North Carolina because of fears that the Rose Bowl in Pasadena could be attacked like Pearl Harbor was three weeks earlier.

team for that decade. Bobby Dodd, the great Georgia Tech coach, called Charley Trippi the greatest all-round football player he'd ever seen. Those days players played offense and defense. Trippi was a great safety man on defense and a great triple-threat tailback on offense. Trippi came back after the war and led us to an undefeated season in 1946. Then, in his first year in professional football, he led the old Chicago Cardinals (not the **BEARS***) to the NFL championship his first year in pro ball. He still lives in Athens. He's almost as old as I am. Sinkwich is dead, but he made a lot of money in the beer distributing business and gave a lot of money to the athletic department.

> Bobby Dodd... called Charley Trippi the greatest all-round football player he'd ever seen.

I saw all the games that fall of 1942, but I had joined the United States Marine Corps, and I was in boot camp at Parris Island, South Carolina. On January 1, the day the team was playing the Rose Bowl, it was a cold day, and I asked one of the drill instructors who had played football at Georgia, Winston Hudson, if he knew where I could get a radio and listen to the game. He said, "I'm going to be listening to the game." He was inside playing cards with some other drill instructors. But, a lowly boot like me—I couldn't go in there and associate with the mighty drill instructors. He said, "When I raise my window, you can be outside my room and listen to the radio from outside." That's what he did. He raised his window a little bit, and I put my head up there. It was freezing cold weather, but I listened to the whole game. We won 9-0.

Winston Hudson, later, was one of the most highly decorated Marines in World War II. On Okinawa, he was a marine platoon leader and he died in action. A few days later, the Japanese surrendered.

*The **CHICAGO BEARS** wear blue and orange because those are the colors that team founder George Halas wore when he played for the University of Illinois.

TIME WELL WASTED

Bob Rushton

Bob Rushton, UGA '66 is retired from his own real estate development and brokerage business in Macon, Georgia. While a student at UGA he was sports editor of The Red & Black *and was replaced by Lewis Grizzard. He is a past president of the Georgia Association of Realtors and was a national president of the United States Jaycees. He served as a judge in the Miss America Pageant in Atlantic City and as a Special U.S. Ambassador under President Carter.*

My earliest memories are coming to games with my dad when I was about six years old. We didn't have tickets. We packed our own lunch and we drove right up next to the stadium along a creek bed, which is now in the Tate Center parking lot. We parked under a big oak tree, got out, ate our lunch, looked around for some tickets and went in the ball game. After the game, we would pick up enough Coca Cola bottles to get the deposits on them. They sold Cokes in the old six-ounce bottles. We would get enough money from the bottles to pay for our trip....

One of my all-time great road games was when we beat Florida 51-0 in the rain. Some people had umbrellas, and the water was running off of them. People would fill their whiskey up with the water running off those umbrellas to have a mixer.

Road trips were a lot of fun. When I was in school, students went on road trips, but not to the extent they go today. Students then didn't have the funds students have now. We'd pile six or eight people in a car and take off if it was a close game like Clemson or South Carolina. Nobody would have any money. Tickets were easy to get. Alumni would give students tickets if they had an extra one. But there wasn't the demand for tickets you have now.

Any place we went, we could get a ticket. There might be one big game a year in the South—say Tennessee and Alabama—that would be sold out. Anything else, a ticket was pretty easy to come by.

When I first came to Athens, the whole county was dry. You could not buy alcohol anywhere. We had to go to Arcade, a little town 13 miles up the road, to get beer. One of the most fun things was to see if we could get past Dean Tate with a bottle in our pockets. I never came close to getting caught, but I had friends who got caught. Back in those days, it was pretty easy to sneak a bottle in. Everybody wore coats and ties to the ball games. Most people took a flask in their hip pocket.

> People would fill their whiskey up with the water running off those umbrellas...

Coach Butts left three or four years before I was a student here. I knew him from watching practices when my dad was in school here. I thought, at the time, he was one of the greatest people I'd ever met, that he was doing what was necessary to have a good football team and teaching the players discipline. By today's standards, he would be considered brutal because he cursed a lot and pushed the guys hard. Coach Butts would personally show the guys how to block and tackle, even though he was a lot smaller than they were. You don't see coaches doing that today. You wouldn't see a coach head-butt a player like Coach Erk Russell. Coach Butts would run them until they dropped. He wanted to make sure they were in condition for the fourth quarter.

I was at a Georgia-Auburn game a few years back. A wasp or a yellow jacket—probably a sorry Georgia Tech yellow jacket—stung this lady in front of me. Everybody got up so they could lay her out on the seats because she had an allergic reaction to being stung. They called the paramedics up, and they took her off to the hospital, but the lady's husband stayed for the second half of the football game. They were with another couple, and they went off to the hospital with her, but the husband stayed. I always wondered what kind of conversation they had later on, but I never did find out.

> ...they took her off to the hospital, but the lady's husband stayed for the second half...

I give grief about as much as I take it at the games. I had a chance to sit with Lewis Grizzard at the last Georgia-Georgia Tech game he went to. He was mad that when we scored the final points to win 48 to something that we didn't **GO FOR TWO*** and make it worse. I was with him 100 percent. I want to beat them as bad as I can every time. The Georgia-Georgia Tech rivalry is just clean, old-fashioned hate. That's pretty close to the way I'd describe it. It's a lot of fun. It's a rivalry the younger generation doesn't understand. Young Georgia fans want to beat Florida. During my lifetime, we beat Florida like a drum. Until Spurrier came, they never beat us.

---

*Ohio State beat Michigan 50-14 in 1968. Ohio State went for a two-point conversion in the fourth quarter. When asked about it, Woody Hayes said, "I WENT FOR TWO because I couldn't go for three."

AGING COMES AT A BAD TIME: 81 IS THE NEW 78:

Marion Pope, Jr.

Marion Pope is 81 years old and lives in Canton, Georgia. He is a former judge, in both the Superior Court and Court of Appeals. He's a "Double Dawg" with a business degree and a law degree from UGA. He graduated in 1953.

I was at Georgia when Athletic Director and Coach Wally Butts was there—he got in trouble with Bear Bryant. This was before technology was what it is today, but someone somehow plugged into a telephone call between Butts and Alabama Coach Bear Bryant before the Georgia-Alabama game. The person who overheard the call accused Bear Bryant and Wally Butts of conspiring to fix the game, which Alabama won 35-0. The story came out in a magazine article after the season. Wally Butts ultimately won a **JUDGMENT*** in court and the magazine settled with Coach Bryant too. They were just talking about football and plays, but it made big news headlines back then.

The stadium was pretty wide open. People took alcohol into the games. It got to be out of control. People behind you would be jumping up and down and their drinks would spill all over you. When people got too rowdy, completely out of control, here'd come the stadium police. If they found someone who was completely out of it, they'd take him out of the game and wouldn't let him back in.

> *When Bear Bryant and Wally Butts won a libel suit and JUDGMENT against the *Saturday Evening Post* years ago, many people conjectured what Bryant and Butts would do with the winnings. Bob Hope suggested that they start a new magazine to compete with *Playboy* called "Bear Butts".

I graduated from Georgia when we still had panty raids. The girls would throw their panties out of the dormitory—we didn't have coed dormitories back then—and the guys would try to catch them. Dean Tate, the legendary dean of men, would walk through the crowd and say, "I know who you are. Give me your ID cards. Give me your ID cards." He'd have a basketful of ID cards. Later you'd get a letter from him telling you to report to his office at a specified time. You'd go in, and he'd say, "Do you want to stay in school?" "Yes sir," was the correct answer. "All right, if I hear of any more of this foolishness, I'm going to write your folks and tell them you're coming home." Nobody wanted to go home. He sure made me stop that "foolishness".

> The person who overheard the call accused Bear Bryant and Wally Butts of conspiring to fix the game...

Several of us would hitchhike to the Georgia-Florida game. We dressed up in school colors, and we'd have a placard, "Gator Bowl or Bust," or something like that. A lot of sympathetic people would pick us up and drive us part of the way to Jacksonville. It wasn't dangerous to pick up hitchhikers then. We would have some money, and all of us would pitch in and get one motel room. We'd sleep on the floor, beds, anywhere. We just wanted to get to the game. We'd try to allow two days to get down. If we could make it in one day, we just partied. We'd always try to find somebody at the game to give us a ride back. "You going back to Athens? You got room?" We'd ask everybody we saw. Sometimes, we would make it to St. Simons Island, where they had a shuttle bus from there even back then. Any way we could get there and back.

When we play Clemson, we have to follow all those little tiger paws on the road to the stadium. Then, as you're driving out of South Carolina, they'll give you a ticket if you have a Georgia tag.

I remember the Georgia Tech-Notre Dame game in Atlanta when the Tech fans carried fish into the stadium and threw them on the field. They threw it for the Catholics who eat fish on Friday. Fish were hitting the football field and bouncing. The referees stopped the game and penalized Coach Dan Devine 15 yards and told him to get off the field. Then, they had to start throwing the fish back off the field so they could resume play. We would never do that at Georgia.

Max Jean-Gilles suffers from Anorexia Ponderosa

WHERE DID THOSE GUYS IN SECTION 105 GO? TRY SECTION 8

William Beck

Beck, 53, is a dentist and lives in Lawrenceville, Georgia.

After a morning of tailgating, we were going into Gate 2, which is always very crowded. My daughter, Nicole, was 15 years old. We were shuffling our way into the stadium pretty close to game time. This elderly couple was making their way in, not something you see every day. They got up against us, so we let them move in front of us. I made a comment to the guy, "Have you been coming to the games a long time? It's nice that you still want to come watch them play." He said, "Oh, I wouldn't miss a game." I made an off-the-cuff comment that it was nice that his wife comes with him. He said, "Wife? This is not my wife. This is my daughter." He said, "I'm 92 years old, and she's 66 years old." She was laughing and said, "I wouldn't miss it." They got separated from us a little bit, and as we are getting to the gate, I looked at my kid and said, "So when I'm that darn old, you're going to be coming to games with me and helping me like this." She said, "Yeah." To me, it was like, "Wow, this is an aspect of Georgia football that people don't understand." Folks have been doing this for a hundred years. Families have been passing their season tickets down—coming with their folks. Then as they've grown up, they've brought their kids.

The away games are more fun for me than home games. I love to go to Auburn or Alabama and walk through their tailgates, hearing them barking mockingly at us. I took my son to Auburn one time. He said, "Dad, they're barking at us!" I said, "That's because they're afraid of us, son." It was Quincy Carter's freshman year. Terry Bowden had been fired. We won.

One year, my season tickets were in section 105. This gal had season tickets right next to me. She didn't the year before or the year after. She brought a different guy to each game. Through the season, you usually see the same people, but with her it was almost like she brought a different potential husband every week, and if he liked Georgia football, she might marry him. She brought this one fellow when we were playing Auburn for one of Coach Donnan's last games. Things weren't going well. Auburn fans had flooded our section. They were even sitting on the steps. You could not get out of your row. About 10-12 rows below us, some Georgia fan was giving a couple of Auburn students what for, to the point that it looked like he wanted to fight. They were trying to get away from him, but it was just too crowded. All this upset a couple of female Auburn fans, who started crying. The security people finally showed up and walked the guy off. Her date leaned over to me and said, "You know there's always one bad apple that spoils the bunch." Before I thought about what I was saying, I looked at him and said, "Ain't nuthin' finer in the land than a drunk, obnoxious Georgia fan." The guy just looked at me. Two or three people sitting around us turned and said, "Go Dawgs!" to him.

> The lady who's crying, she should have taken her purse and beaned the Georgia fan over the head.

This poor Yankee was from Syracuse, New York. I said, "You haven't been to too many SEC games. This is like a family fight." He said, "Don't you think that was classless to make those ladies cry?" I said, "Well, it's probably no more classless than when they turned the fire hoses on our fans after we beat them at Auburn a couple of years ago." He said, "What?" I said, "See, you don't know. I know a lot of Auburn fans, and I'm friends with them.

Monday morning, we'll be laughing. People who go to these games, they understand. The lady who's crying, she should have taken her purse and beaned the Georgia fan over the head. That would have been expected." He didn't get it—he really didn't. I was looking at the gal. She looked up at the sky and said, "All right. This one's off my list, too."

Georgia football is a source of pride. We're used to seeing our teams give it their all. We're used to being proud of them and reading stories about how some of them go on to be doctors or work in vineyards or go pro. When the rest of the world thinks we're a bunch of idiots, we know we're not. Our guys prove it in the toughest conference in the world.

Phil Fulmer looks just like Brad Pitt except totally different.

MAYBE THAT WAS JUST
EFFIE'S WAY OF SAYING "HELLO"

Bill Shipp

*Shipp has been working in Georgia journal-
ism for over 50 years. He served as managing
editor of* The Red & Black *while attending the
University of Georgia. He went into the Army
and later returned home to begin working at
the* Atlanta Journal Constitution. *Today, he is a syndicated columnist and a panelist on the TV program "The Georgia Gang." He
lives in Acworth, Georgia.*

I got a lot of praise for my efforts to integrate the University of
Georgia in the '50s but my prize project was one I lost. During
my student days at *The Red & Black* I campaigned mightily
with the pen to close down Effie's. Most young readers have
never heard of Effie's and older readers will claim never to have
heard of it. Effie's was a house of ill fame which served Athens for
many, many years. Effie's clientele were said to be prominent cit-
izens of Athens...and about half the male population of the
University of Georgia. It operated for many years under the noses
of city fathers. As hard as I tried, I failed to close down Effie's and
it continued for some 20 years after I left only to succumb in the
1970s when the amateur competition of the "free love " era wiped
it out. I am sure that the mere mention of Effie's may bring a smile
to some older readers faces...or, maybe it won't!

I remember the first time I went to football practice and watched
Coach Wally Butts work the team. I was shocked. Here was this
little bitty guy who would hit on these big guys, push them around
and dare them to hit him back. They wouldn't get close to him.

I'd left *The Red & Black* long before Coach Dooley arrived. I got to
know him fairly well and found him to be a very scholarly man

and a great conversationalist. I enjoyed talking to him about entering politics and finding out how interesting he really was. I enjoyed being around him. While I was a student, Georgia football didn't mean a lot to me. Later, it came to mean a good deal, particularly after Dooley came. I thought there was a different kind of atmosphere on the football field and Coach Dooley was a different sort than they'd ever had there before.

Fred Davidson, a former Georgia president, and I had not always been the best of friends. One year, shortly before he left, he invited me to sit with him in the President's box at a football game. We had been adversaries because of contradictory journalistic ideas—he definitely wasn't a big fan of newspapers.

Jan Kemp was an instructor at Georgia, whose contract was not renewed because of her criticism of the athletes' developmental studies program. She blew the whistle on the university and caused a huge uproar. I later discovered that she lived in a subdivision near my home. When I tried to meet with her to get her side of the story she refused. She would, however, leave statements for me in her mailbox and I'd come and get them myself and use them to write my stories. I could see her in her house peeping around the shades when I would come by. It was a huge scandal over Georgia's athletic programs at the time. It resulted in Fred Davidson being forced to resign. She also sued the university and won a financial settlement and got her job back. Georgia became a leader in reforming what were then common practices.

BEER: MORE THAN A BREAKFAST DRINK

Gary Tolbert

Tolbert, 58, is a '71 graduate of UGA and is the president of Airways Event Freight Group in DeSoto, Texas.

In 1969, Georgia was playing Tulane, our first game of the season. Georgia wound up winning the game 35-0. It was extremely hot—mid 90s and the humidity was way up there. Georgia had a really good season in 1968 so everybody was expecting great things of the football team. The mood in the stadium was festive and every time Georgia scored, and it seemed like they scored every time they had the ball, the whole crowd would chant, "Damn Good Team! Damn Good Team! Damn Good Team!" over and over again. The heat was just unbearable and late in the game, there was just one cloud in the sky. It came over us just enough to block the sun from the entire stadium. Every one in the stadium, not only the Georgia fans, but the Tulane fans—the few that were there, began to chant, "Damn Good Cloud! Damn Good Cloud! Damn Good Cloud!" because we got a little bit of relief from the sun. Because the heat was so miserable, that cloud became the memorable part of the day for me....

When I started school in '67, everyone wore coats and ties to the football games. We played Tennessee in Athens my junior year. We had all gotten dressed up and were on our way to the game. About an hour before the game, the rain started—just pouring down rain. Everybody ran back to their dorms and apartments and took their coats and ties off and threw on jeans and sweatshirts. From then on...that's what we wore to games. That rainy day against Tennessee ended our having to get dressed up with coats and ties to go to football games....

When I moved to Dallas, Texas in 1981, there was the University of Georgia, North Texas Alumni Association—this was long before the Internet. We used to get with the Alumni Association to listen to the games. In those days you would call up long distance to someone in Athens who would then place the telephone by the radio so we could listen to Larry Munson call the game. That was the only way we could get a play by play and hear what was going on at the game. It was rather complicated, we had a long distance phone call...a telephone placed by a radio...a telephone laid in front of a microphone at a bar...and then the live broadcast over the bar's loud speakers! Terrible sound, but that's all we could do back then.

The University of Georgia, North Texas Alumni Association gets together for every Georgia game. Now with satellite TV, we get to watch the games whenever they're broadcast on any satellite station. The bar where we go is in Irving, Texas. It's not reserved totally for us but about half the bar on a football Saturday will be Georgia alumni. There'll be other TVs in there turned to Big 12 or Southwest Conference *way back then* games. If somebody comes in wearing another jersey, we're pretty brutal on them. They may be coming in to watch Texas, or whoever. Both my kids went to A&M so we're Aggie fans, too. But, on Georgia game day, we want everybody to be dressed in red and black. Occasionally we'll get an opponent who comes in to watch the game. That's really interesting. We're quite friendly. We're not mean to them by any means, but if Georgia wins, they know they're in the wrong place. Georgia doesn't have mean fans, at least not that I know of. Some schools are just known to be mean, but Georgia isn't. We welcome, but we get our two cents worth in.

Since I graduated from Georgia in '71, which was a long time ago, there have been a lot of highs and lows. We used to have a saying when I was there that we needed Vince Dooley like we needed a case of his initials. Everybody's an Uga fan. I've got Uga pictures all around my house. I've got Uga more than I do Georgia football pictures of players. Uga is universal—Uga is ongoing—players come and go.

When I was in school, Mike Cavan was the quarterback. He later became the head coach at SMU. Cavan got kicked out of the athletic dorm for shooting a BB gun at people playing tennis on the open courts, which were close to the athletic dorm. I was a residence assistant in one of the dorms. Cavan got moved into my dormitory. About three o'clock one morning, I was awakened to hear all this noise out in the hallway. I went out there and saw a door close but I didn't see anybody. I went down and knocked on the door and this guy I didn't know opened the door. But, it was Mike Cavan's room. I said, "Hey guys, be quiet, don't make such a ruckus." I went back to my room, closed the door and about two-three minutes later, a broad arrow hit my door. I know who shot it, but I couldn't prove it. By the time I got out there, they were gone.

Back in those days, there was no drinking on campus. Residence assistants, after football games, would hide in the bushes and catch people getting six packs of beer out of their cars. Then, you'd go down and take them to student court before the dean of men. It was a big deal back then but now people would laugh at something like that.

We knew there was one particular dormitory where they were having parties. We had to pull this undercover sort of thing to get invited in to get somebody to offer you a beer. If that happened, you would raise the shade and then the dean of men and the campus police would show up at the door. I'm the one. I'd go in. I'd find the beer. I raised the shade. At my signal everybody shows up. There's a bunch of people in the room who all get taken down to campus police headquarters, me included, because they didn't want anybody to know I was the one. It turns out that, as the story is told, the guy whose room we were in—his father was in the mafia or something in New York, and he's running around campus saying that for ten bucks, whoever it was that told on them, they could have killed. *Over a case of beer!*

Another RA and I are hiding in the bushes one night after a game. Two or three guys open their car trunk and are getting a couple of cases of beer out. We jump out of the bushes and yell. They go running off. We're chasing them, and then we realize, "What the heck are we going to do if we catch them? There's two of us—there's three of them. We went, "This is stupid." We turned around and walked back cause we're chasing after guys we can't do anything with if we get hold of them. So we went back to their car and had a beer!

The world was different the last time Mississippi State won the title... for one thing, it was flat.

SHORT STORIES FROM LONG MEMORIES

In 1977, Prince Charles visited the University of Georgia for a football game. He came at halftime. He walked out on the field to shake hands with people and to wave to the fans. It was funny, because the fans had a lot of homemade banners made out of bed sheets. Most of them said something like, "Will You Marry Me?" or "I Love You, Prince Charles." One of the banners said, "Prince Charles Does It Dawg-Style," tying him into our Bulldog theme. It was such a fun game and, of course, something a little different.

In the late 1970s, the University of Alabama was a real powerhouse in the South. Everybody wanted to beat them because they never lost. They had their 'Roll Tide' slogan every time the ball was kicked off. We didn't have anything at that time. For a couple of weeks everyone had been trying to decide on a good slogan for Georgia's kickoffs. Finally someone came up with, "Go Dawgs." I don't know if they still say it or not but, at the time, they would yell "Go Dawgs!" As that trailed off, everyone would yell, "Sic 'em!" We did that all through the Alabama game in '76, and won 21-0. We completely shut them out. That night we spent most of the evening driving up and down Milledge Avenue. Everybody was honking and waving and, of course, drinking a little bit of alcohol. There were people on top of roofs, people on top of cars and street lights just partying...having a great time. We were thrilled that we'd beat them—not just beat them, but shut them out...

> In 1977, Prince Charles visited the University of Georgia for a football game.

—CINDY KOZLOWSKI, UGA '79, Rochester Hills, Michigan

Sanford Stadium had been selected as an Olympic venue for the 1996 **OLYMPIC GAMES***. In 1995, the Auburn game was the last

> *The first **OLYMPICS** ever held in North America were in St. Louis in 1904. It was also the first Olympics where gold, silver, and bronze medals were awarded.

game of the season and following the game they were going to tear down the hedges to prepare the field for Olympic soccer events. A buddy of mine and I went down to the field after the game was over and decided we wanted to take some of the hedges home with us. We broke off small pieces of a hedge. This is not the year the hedges were trampled—this was completely different.

Then we saw some other people pulling up the hedges. For the next 30 minutes, we worked on this piece of hedge trying to pull it up. Finally, we got the whole thing up, including the root ball. We wrapped it in wet paper towels and put it in a plastic bag. We took it back to my parents' house, and I look at it every day knowing that this hedge is the same exact hedge that the Bulldogs played in front of all those years. If we ever move to another house, that hedge will move with us!

We call it the 'junior varsity hedge' because after the Olympics they went back in and replanted all the hedges. So, we consider ours the JV hedge. For months after that, Krogers and other places around Athens were selling hedges that came out of Sanford Stadium. They rooted them and were growing them in little pots, and you could get a certificate of authenticity. But, shoot, we just went down and got it ourselves. It was a lot more fun to pull it out of the ground than it was to go buy it in a pot. We don't need a certificate. We know it's real....

—KEVIN TALLANT, 31, Cumming, Ga.

Growing up, my father deemed it inappropriate to go to a football game because of the money it cost, the crowds and all that stuff. We would religiously sit around the radio and listen to Larry Munson every Saturday. I liked his pessimism! It's almost annoying, but, at the same time, it gets you fired up. You can tell the true passion in his voice about football and Georgia....

My wife Melissa got us student tickets. Since she was in the band she didn't have to use hers, so we gave it to a buddy of mine, Jay, a Florida State fan. It was his first time to a Georgia game. We were standing underneath the bridge by the Dawg Walk waiting for the band to start when a car pulled up right next to us. We didn't think anything about it until they opened the hatchback and there in his little carrier was Uga. Nobody was around, so Jay stuck his finger into the cage. I said, "Hey, that's probably not a good idea. That is a bulldog." He said, "Oh, but he's so cute and loveable." I said, "No, I'm serious. I think he might bite your finger." He stuck his finger right in the cage. Uga, without growling or anything just opened his mouth and bit him. He just held there for a second. Jay held his finger there for the longest time and then said, "This is so cool. Uga's biting me." He pulled his hand back. The bite had just barely broken the skin on top—it was like a little love bite. He took pictures of his hand, and he took pictures of Uga. I don't think Uga's owner saw us do it, but I'm sure he would have been ticked off if he did. Jay will always remember his first UGA trip when Uga bit him....

> Every time I smell bourbon and Coke and vomit, I think of Georgia games.

One time I was walking down the ramps on the backside where the tracks are. This old lady, probably in her late 60s, was sitting there singing, "It's great to be a Georgia Bulldog." Then she stopped for a second, leaned on the railing and threw up. Every time I smell bourbon and Coke and vomit, I think of Georgia games.

—RUSTY PARKER, 24, Navy recruiter in Chattanooga

My wife and I both retired from the University of Georgia. Years ago, when my wife was talking to a lady about a job interview, I said, "Hey, Baby, hang on a minute, ask them if we're going to be able to get football tickets." She's talking salary, and I'm talking football tickets. We did get the tickets. That was the beginning....

We moved to Morganton when we retired and now I leave early Friday morning for home games in Athens. I don't know whether the university would like it if they knew I slept in my truck, but I did. I didn't think I was getting there early enough. On Friday nights, a lot of people used to come and tailgate. They didn't care. You could start doing whatever you wanted to do at five or six o'clock on Friday afternoon back in those days. The university changed that. Now you can't start tailgating until 7 a.m. Saturday. On game-day mornings, everybody is there, all the people you know. It's amazing how you make so many friends down through the years.

I've been a Georgia fan forever. The first time I ever went to Sanford Stadium, we sat up in the nose-bleed section. It was awesome. Even though we were sitting up high, we could get the whole view and see the plays developing. I tell people whenever I go to the game, if Georgia's being defeated on the field, to me, it feels like I'm watching somebody beat up on my kids, and I can't do anything about it. It means a lot to me and I just want to get out there and help them.

> ...Georgia's being defeated on the field, it feels like I'm watching somebody beat up on my kids...

The last time Georgia won the SEC championship, I loved it. They weren't expected to go very far that year. Pat Dye said, "Georgia's not man enough to beat Auburn." After the game Danny West got a sign off the side of the wall at the stadium. He ran around the field with that sign, "We're mad about it. We're mad about it." I loved it. Somebody asked him what he was going to do with that sign. He said, "I'm putting it in my room." He was not going to part with that sign, and I'm glad.

—WAYNE SAYLORS, 73, Morganton, Ga., retired

One of the most interesting things that happened during the years I was in the band was when we stopped playing "Dixie." For some reason, "Dixie" was considered as much a part of the Georgia fight song as anything else we would play. We couldn't go to a game without somebody, hollering, "I want to hear 'Dixie.'" Sometimes when we were playing in the stands, we would have to play "Dixie." The year they decided to stop, the band director really caught it from the fans. There were *Red & Black* editorials about it. They wanted the band director to know that it was a terrible thing that the band wouldn't play "Dixie," anymore. They even used to call us the Dixie Redcoat band. There was some tension that became an issue among many people in the segregated South. They ended up dropping Dixie off the name and stopped playing the song. Since that day, I don't guess the band has ever played Dixie. I enjoyed marching into the stadium with the band and everybody cheering. After the game, we'd play a little concert while the fans were leaving. Sometimes over a thousand people would stay to hear us, particularly if it had been a great victory. That was always my favorite part of the game.

The biggest thing I remember about Jacksonville is the parties and all the people drinking. In a way, it has become more of a spectacle. It's almost taken the fun out of it because people are just too inebriated and are almost out of control. After the game, even when Georgia has won, when you're leaving the stadium, the Florida fans are shouting out the years they've won. They still count off all those years.

For me going to Georgia was fun. College was the first time I'd spent four years in one place. It was a special time for me, making friends and getting to go to the games and to the Sugar Bowl and the Liberty Bowl. Back in those days, the Cotton Bowl was one of the major bowls, and we got to go there so it was a truly, truly wonderful time.

—RAYMOND PATRICIO, 62, Savannah, Georgia

I was born and raised in Athens and graduated from Georgia in 1974. I grew up in the stadium, sold programs, used to play football for the YMCA before the Georgia football games. My grandfather was one of many community members who had to sign a guarantee for the loan when Sanford Stadium was being built. As a reward for that, they let those people have their first pick of seats in the stadium. After Georgia won the national championship, they raised the contribution level so much that they allowed those people, for the first time, to pass their seats down to their children. My father had inherited them from my grandfather, and then my mother was able to give the tickets to us, so we still sit in those same seats.

We always seem to get seated near a group of students. It's amazing to me how many students come in, and, by the time they get to the game, they are so totally over-served that they don't make it through the end of the game. It's interesting because usually one of them will pass out and then that person will rally and another one will have a sinking spell and then that one will rally and then the other one. We watch them go in and out all game long. To me, it's as much fun as the game—trying to predict whether they're going to make it or not. I wonder if any of them ever even remember the game.

—RUSTY GUNN, 55, attorney, Macon, Georgia

The Georgia-Georgia Tech rivalry is fantastic. Whoever wins, gets bragging rights the whole year at the Rotary Clubs and things like that. God help us, if we lose. They really lay it into us. It's a lot of good, clean, old-fashioned hate.

> ...it was a big electrical transformer— it wasn't a bathroom at all.

We go to the Georgia-Florida game every year. It used to be pretty open with alcohol, but they're tightening it down. After one of the games, there was a big line to go to the restroom. We noticed people ahead of us would leave the line. We finally got up to the bathroom and looked in—it was a big electrical transformer—it wasn't a bathroom at all. We might have had a little too much to drink because we almost got a big shock!

When I was a student, it was pretty easy to sneak booze into the stadium. The ladies would just put it in their pocketbooks. We would go with these little half-pints of bourbon. You can't do that today. We didn't have all the terrible things that have happened lately, people behaved themselves pretty well. I support that we probably should restrict the alcohol. That was an earlier—more innocent—time when we just had it all.

—NEELY YOUNG, Marietta, 66, UGA '65

The mood of the crowd is a very addictive thing. It bleeds onto you. I know a lot about football. I can read what the refs are doing down there, and I can call some plays. I've taken people who never even saw a football before. One time I brought an Italian, two Spaniards, and a Brazilian; it was a motley crew, and I got all of them to go to a game with me. I made sure they had their red shirts. We tailgated. I really wanted to show them honestly how we did it—start to finish. I didn't want to just hand them tickets and say, "Meet me in the game." We cooked out. I had bratwursts, hamburgers, and a keg. They really appreciated it. They said,

"We don't get it, but we're having a good time." They don't do all that for **SOCCER*** games.

We arrived just in time for the "Star Spangled Banner." Everybody stands up and takes off their hats, and the singing is very solemn. After it was over, my friend, Jose turned to me and said, "Wow! We don't do that in Spain. In Spain, if you heard somebody singing the national anthem you would think they were fascist or ultra-nationalists." I laughed and said, "Sometimes we get that way a little bit." He said, "No, I'm serious. That is really, really cool." He became very emotional. He said that, to him, that was almost a religious experience, just watching all these people, many of us, other than Georgia football, had nothing in common except for the fact that we were all Americans and were all darn proud to be Americans. That was really something special. Jose was a very humble guy, who had never bragged about his family. His father helped write the Spanish constitution after Franco died in the seventies. He was a member of the Spanish Parliament. He ended up being a member of the European Parliament, and now is a professor in Madrid. Jose didn't just come from Spain. He had a pretty good education. He spoke four languages.

Football is a religion in the South. When we're all in that stadium cheering the same team on, it is an incredible feeling. We do the National Anthem and then, directly afterward, we do "Glory". There's the trumpeter in the corner of the stadium doing the first bars to "Glory, Glory," and Larry Munson's voice comes on, and that is really incredible. At that moment, everyone in the stadium is tied together on two-tiers. They're tied together for their patriotism, and they're tied together for their love of the game. It's muggy. The humidity in late summer is disgusting. If it's sunny you get good and sunburned but I wouldn't trade it for anything.

—MATTHEW FOSTER, 23 Cedartown, Georgia

> *More U.S. kids today play **SOCCER** than any other organized sport, including youth football. Perhaps, the reason so many kids play soccer is so they don't have to watch it.

Back in our college days, we'd put a pint bottle in our sport coat pockets. Back then, you had to wear a coat and tie and buy a big pom pon (Most people incorrectly say pom pom) or flower for your date to wear. Those were college days.

I bought a red and black Blazer back in the early eighties and drove it until I got my first motor home in 1990. From then on, it was motor homes until the UGA president decided he didn't want us leaving our trash around, so he put us all off campus. I still have a real ugly spot in my mind for them making us quit parking motor homes on university property, except for one little section that the Bulldog Club controls. The cleanest places on the campus were where the motor homes were. It was always clean when we left there on Sunday morning. You could tell where the regular car tailgaters were and where the motor homes had been parked. I got rid of my motor home because I can't put it on the University of Georgia campus.

—EDMUND CHARLES INMAN, 75, Macon, UGA '52

> The cleanest places on the campus were where the motor homes were.

I proposed to my wife Laura on a Wednesday in October, 1977, the weekend before Georgia was to play Kentucky. It was also the game when Prince Charles visited the University and was greeted by the crowd at halftime. Laura was a member of the Flag Corps that year and was on the field. I was standing on the sidelines looking over the hedges as the Prince came out at halftime. Laura's parents were sitting in their seats on the other side of the stadium. As the Prince walked down between a receiving line of University of Georgia majorettes, auxiliary corps and band, he stopped and talked with a couple of the girls along the way. At one point, he stopped and talked to Laura, and afterwards, I asked her what he had said. She said he asked her what team she was cheering for. She answered, "Georgia, of course." What made the question funny was the fact that she was dressed in a Georgia band uniform, was holding a red and black flag and was standing with the group of Georgia Redcoat band members. I remember watching from the sidelines as he went over and spoke to her. I believe he also kissed her on the cheek, and then he walked on. My mother-in-law who is a big camera buff had a camera trained on the field and was able to take one or two photographs of him close to Laura. It was a big event overshadowed later that day by a 33-0 loss to Kentucky.

Back in the days when Sanford was double-tiered and open on both ends, one of the favorite places for fans to sit for games was on the railroad track 'cause you could easily see into the stadium from there. Occasionally, a train would come and all those people who had built their temporary seats on the tracks to watch the game would have to scurry off the tracks quickly. The train would go by and then all of them would fight to try to get back to where they had been sitting before. It was a funny break in the action because everybody in the stadium, including the teams, would turn and watch all these people run off the railroad tracks to avoid the train and then the mad scramble to get their places back. I always sat inside the stadium and loved to watch that scene when a train came by.

—PAUL MCKOWN, UGA '75, Marietta, GA

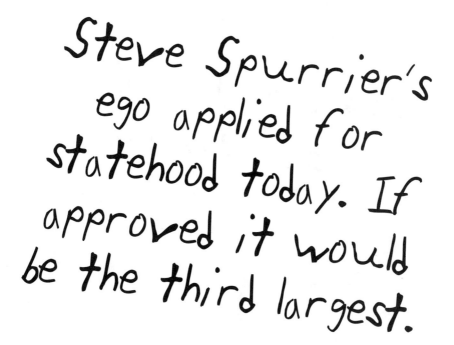

Steve Spurrier's ego applied for statehood today. If approved it would be the third largest.

Tallahassee has a Win Chill factor.

Flush twice— it's a long way to Gainesville!

Chapter 4

A Hard Way to Make an Easy Living

Buenos Noches, Coaches

A COACH IS A TEACHER
WITH A DEATH WISH

Ray Goff

Ray Goff, 52, quarterbacked the Bulldogs '74-'76. He was SEC Player of the Year and finished seventh in the Heisman Trophy voting in '76. He replaced Vince Dooley as head football coach at the age of 33 following the 1988 season. He finished his career as head coach with an overall record of 46-31-1. He is presently in the real estate and restaurant business with Zaxby Restaurants in Georgia and Alabama.

I'm from a little town in south Georgia called Moultrie. Two people recruited me, Sterling Dupree, who has since passed on, and Pat Hodgson. I was recruited by quite a few other schools, but those are the two gentlemen who recruited me here at Georgia. The decision came down to the fact that I really liked Pat Hodgson more than anyone else. At one point, I thought about going to Tennessee, but I felt that Coach Bill Battle, the assistant coach and recruiter, was trying to push me into making a commitment I wasn't ready to make. I scratched Tennessee off and started leaning toward Georgia. I am tickled to death that I did because I have a lot of great friends from Athens. I'm sure I would have had some from Tennessee as well, but I really enjoyed my association with the people here in the state of Georgia. This is where I'm from. This is where I've lived my whole life.

One of the greatest games I was involved in, one that was a total team victory, was when we shut out Alabama, 21-0, in 1976. It was the first time in 66 games that Coach Bryant had been shut out. After the game, the streets in Athens were shut down. They had bands at all the fraternity houses. It's the most excitement

I've ever seen in this town. It started on Thursday before the game and built up all week and through the weekend.

Playing for the national championship is nice. Except, we lost in '82 to Penn State. I remember that Bourbon Street was wild. We couldn't go outside because there were so many people everywhere. They all wanted to talk to us and hug us and wish us luck. Then, we went and got beat, and nobody wanted to talk us. So, after the game, we didn't have a problem.

> Dooley snatched a wig off his head. He had shaved his head bald!

One of the best memories I have of Coach Dooley was our '76 team. Before the season started, a bunch of our players, 20 or so of them, shaved their heads bald. Every week that we won, a coach said he would shave his head. Coach Dooley said if we won all the games and played for a championship he would shave his. We lost one game that year—we were 10-1. Almost our whole coaching staff was bald. At the end of the season we had a coronation banquet where everybody—alumni, friends, Touchdown Club—got together. At the banquet Coach Dooley snatched a wig off his head. He had shaved his head bald! There are a lot of heads that need hair—his was one of them.

During my coaching years we had a good group of players. They were probably underrated to some degree because they all, for the most part, have been very successful in the business world or in pro football. The great thing about coaching is when players come back and say, "Coach, I understand what you tried to teach me. I've got my own children, and I understand." When they call and ask for advice, it makes me realize they appreciate me. I couldn't be prouder of a group of guys than the ones I was fortunate enough to be around—blessed to be around.

I recruited Bill Goldberg, who was quite a character and is now a famous wrestler. I enjoyed him and loved his family. They were just great people. I don't see Bill as much today, but I do keep up with his family. Bill was a rounder. He liked to have a good time. When he came to Athens for his recruiting visit, we had a linebacker named Steve Boswell, who took Bill out. After he went out with Boswell for the weekend, he committed to us telling us he was coming to Georgia. I didn't ask where they went or what they did because I didn't want to know. I just know he had a good time. Bill continued to have a good time at Athens, Georgia until the day he left.

I remember when we flew down to Valdosta and Albany to get new recruits Greg Talley and David Hargett. We were on a **SMALL PLANE*** about to take off from Albany, and the plane's engine wouldn't kick over. These recruits had never flown before. The pilot got a little hammer and hit the engine in a certain place, got back in and cranked the engine up. Those boys looked at me like we were flying a crop-duster. They were scared to death.

Georgia football—it's not the game, it's the people. I got fired here, but this is still my state and still my home. I love the University of Georgia. It's been very good to me, very kind to me. Georgia people, they're the best.

---

*During his long career, Florida State coach Bobby Bowden was offered the head coaching jobs at Marshall University and LSU. Bowden eventually turned down both opportunities...the two coaches who accepted those positions were both killed in job-related **PLANE** crashes.

IT TOOK A LOT OF BALLS

Tom Cloud

Tom Cloud is a graduate of the University of Georgia Business School and is a financial advisor. His son Tom Jr. went astray and graduated from Georgia Tech.

I was the football team's student manager in 1968 and 1969; I traveled with the team and was down on the field with them. When we traveled, I drove the big equipment truck. I left on Thursday nights and arrived early Friday mornings. The players would arrive later that day. We'd have to have everything ready so the players could go in and walk the field.

The equipment managers would be ball boys during games. We'd have one ball boy on each of the sidelines. We were responsible for Georgia's footballs. When the Georgia quarterback threw an incomplete pass, I would hand a new ball to the referee and chase the other ball down. When the opposing team had the ball, we would sit down. Their ball boys would get their balls. They didn't want us touching their footballs.

I was a freshman when **ARCHIE MANNING*** and Ole Miss came to Athens in 1968. Ole Miss had us shut out at halftime. Obviously, our offense hadn't played very well. The defense played really well except for a couple of lapses. I had heard Coach Erk Russell in practice, and seen his intensity, but that halftime was the first time I'd ever really seen him in action during a game. I

> *...**ARCHIE MANNING** has the worst winning percentage in NFL history of QBs with 100+ starts...Author John Grisham lived in Oxford, Mississippi at one time. In Grisham's book *The Pelican Brief* there was a character named Justice Archibald Manning. In his book *A Time to Kill* there is a poster of Archie Manning.

don't even remember exactly what he said, but I do remember how he said it. The players knew they were going to go out there and win that game. We killed Ole Miss in the second half. It was the fourth game of the season, and we went on to win the SEC championship that year.

Managers took turns driving Coach Dooley to his TV Show. I drove him several times over a two-year period. We would take him in his red and black Riviera. I'd pick the Riviera up on Saturday night and pick him up on Sunday morning at his house. He filmed his shows at WSD. After the show, I joined him for Sunday lunch with different alumni. I was only 18 years old, and I was driving Coach Dooley to film his TV show and having lunch with pretty influential alumni. That was a really good feeling.

The thing I loved about Coach Dooley is that he gave me respect, and I gave him respect. He didn't have to tell you to respect him; you respected him because he practiced what he preached. He worked hard. He wasn't a yeller or screamer, but he was very intense. He wanted to win. In high school, I had coaches who would jump on me and try to belittle me, but I never saw that from Coach Dooley. If a player was dragging and wasn't trying, he said something to him, but he never tried to belittle anybody. He always respected people. Even today, I'll see him, and he'll ask about my children and grandchildren. He's genuinely interested in everybody who played or worked hard for him.

My most vivid memory is from 1957. I was seven years old. Theron Sapp scored the game's only touchdown and Georgia won 7-0. My father, who was a very serious guy, broke down. It was unbelievable. Georgia had beaten Tech after eight years. Bulldog fans call that game the "drought breaker."

In 1959, my father and I were down on the sidelines during the game when Georgia beat Auburn for the SEC championship. My mom would have gone to the game but she stayed home with my younger brother and sister. After I got home, I got a little agitated and said a cussword. My mom said, "Where in the world did you hear that?" I said, "Coach Butts said that on the sideline today." I never got to sit on the sidelines again.

CULTURAL LEARNINGS OF COACHES FOR MAKE BENEFIT GLORIOUS BULLDOG NATION

Bruce Yawn

Bruce Yawn, 60, lives in Statesboro, Georgia, and owns Snooky's restaurant, a very popular gathering place for Georgia Southern and Georgia folks. He played guard for Georgia from 1965 through 1968.

My daddy wanted me to go to Tech for some reason. That might be why I chose Georgia. I liked the coaching staff. I seemed to be the right fit for them, more than anything else.

Years later, I own a restaurant in Statesboro. After Coach Erk Russell had come to Georgia Southern to be head coach, we were sitting at a table talking. He asked me, "Did you ever think about quitting when you were a player?" I said, "I thought about it every day." He said, "Why didn't you?" I said, "I didn't have the guts to quit." I had never quit anything in my life. I asked him, "Did you ever think about it?" He said, "I kept my bags packed for a whole week one time while I was at Auburn." I think all of us have been through that. There were some days when I didn't think we were going to make it through practice. We tend to forget those times, though.

I really didn't get to know Coach Russell until he came to Georgia Southern. I played offensive guard, and he was defensive coach. We could tell there was something special about him because the defensive players would always come out of their meetings laughing. He was always telling jokes.

I worked very closely with getting football here at Southern. When we first started talking about bringing football here, the president of Georgia Southern had made up his mind that he wanted to bring it. He was holding breakfast meetings at the college—it was not even a university back then—to talk to local business people about football. He had promised the Georgia Southern Foundation that he would not actively solicit money from anybody in Statesboro for football. They felt that would hurt the giving for other Georgia Southern programs.

At one of the meetings I attended, the president said, "I want to remind you that I promised the foundation I would not solicit money in Statesboro." Cy Waters, who has a furniture store in town, and I were at church after one of those meetings. I remember standing at the back and talking about how we both would love to see football at Georgia Southern. Both of us made the same comment. "He said he wouldn't raise money, but he didn't say that *we* couldn't raise money."

> I told my wife, "I cannot believe that Coach Russell would be interested in coming here."

So, we got about six or eight people together to talk about it. We ran an article in the paper that said we were holding a meeting at the high school cafeteria for anybody interested in football at Georgia Southern. We had about 150 people at that meeting. We came up with a two-year giving plan. We divided a list up and started talking to people. That was in '79. We soon discovered there was a lot of interest in football and people were willing to support it.

When we first started talking about it, to be honest with you, most of us were thinking Division III or Division II. Then Coach Russell's name popped up as someone interested in the head coach position. One night I told my wife, "I cannot believe that Coach Russell would be interested in coming here."

I called him to talk about what I was hearing. I felt funny calling him because I didn't know him that well. I said, "I keep hearing your name pop up, that you are interested in this job." But he would never answer a question. He'd always answer by asking another question. He said, "What do you think about it?" I said,

"Well, to be honest with you, it's a win-win situation for me. Of course, I played at Georgia, and my heart's in Georgia, but I make my living here at Georgia Southern in Statesboro. It would be great." He said, "What do you think about recruiting?" I said, "I think recruiting would be good." He said, "What do you think about the support down there?" He never said he was interested in the job. When we got off the phone, I told my wife, "He's interested in this job." He just asked questions. Until the day he died, that's the way he was. You had to pull things out of him.

Once he was coming, we never thought about Division III or Division II again. His name gave us instant credibility.

Coach Russell acted like just one of the guys, but to everybody, he was like a rock star. People loved being around him. Every restaurant in every town has a coffee group—one or two tables where 40 or 50 different people will come in and out every morning. My restaurant has that, too. That's where Erk would sit. After a while, folks started treating him like one of the guys.

All he had to do was mention something—he never had to ask for anything. One day he was sitting in my restaurant, right across from campus, and he said, "That field on the edge of campus would be a great place to have a practice field." It happened that one of the guys sitting with him was in the grass business. Another guy was in the irrigation business. The irrigation guy got somebody to donate the irrigation, and he did the work. The other guy got somebody to help him. Of course, they already had the field there, but they went in there and worked it over. The next thing you know it's a great field. All Coach Russell had to do was mention it.

Another day, the subject of cocaine came up. Somebody made the comment, "I tell you what, that stuff is more deadly than a rattlesnake." It was about the time Coach Russell was preparing to give a drug talk to the players. He asked, "Where could I get my hands on a rattlesnake?" Jim Tillman, one of the guys said, "I've got a friend with the Department of Natural Resources. Let me call him." Two or three days later, I heard them talking, and Coach Russell said, "I need to have it here Thursday night."

Thursday night a guy from DNR walked in to my restaurant and said, "I've got a rattlesnake here." I said, "Rattlesnake!" "Yes. The one for Coach Russell." I said, "Wait just a minute." I called Coach Russell, and he told me where at the college he wanted the guy with the rattlesnake to meet him. He had all the players in a room, talking about drugs. When the guy got to the meeting, Erk was telling them to stay away from drugs. Finally, Erk said, "Drugs are more deadly than a rattlesnake." He called in the DNR guy and said, "Put that thing on the table." Erk Russell poured that rattlesnake out on the table, and about ten of the players ran out of the room. Erk screamed at them, "Get back in here! That's exactly what I want y'all to do if you ever run into anybody you know is using drugs, get out of there just like that." He had a knack for making a point.

A large ditch runs right through Erk's practice field. He called it 'Beautiful Eagle Creek.' When it rained, it would have some water in it. The team was getting ready to leave for a playoff game, and it was raining. Coach Russell asked me if I had a milk jug. I said, "What do you want with a milk jug?" He said, "I want to take some of that Beautiful Eagle Creek water and sprinkle it in the opponent's end zone. I'll tell the players that the mystical powers of Beautiful Eagle Creek will keep their team from scoring." I said, "It's raining. I'll take a milk jug and get you some." He said, "No, you'll just go back there and fill it with tap water." He took a milk jug, drove over there in the rain and got actual water out of the creek. He got on the plane and held the jug between his legs. I don't think anybody had any idea what it was. When the got to where they were going and were practicing before the game, he got them all down in the end zone and told them all about the Eagle Creek water. He made a ceremony out of sprinkling that water in the end zone. They won the game. Now, there's a granite marker beside Beautiful Eagle Creek. He would take something really small and make something really big out of it.

One of the funniest stories I ever heard was when Coach Russell was sitting over here one morning about six o'clock. I asked, "What are you doing up so early?" He said, "I've got one of my boys out there running." It was still dark. He could sit in here and watch the practice field across the street. He said, "You want to know what happened?" I nodded. "He broke one of my rules." The only rule Erk had was 'do right.' Erk would determine what was right and what was wrong. He said the boy got caught with a girl in his room. Erk called all the players up and said, "I've got some good news, and I've got some bad news. What do you want to hear first?" They said, "We want to hear the bad news." He said, "Well, so and so

> "The good news is that if he can get a girl in his room, any of y'all can."

broke one of the rules." They said, "Oooh. What did he do?" He said, "He got caught with a girl in his room, and he's going to have to be punished for it." They said, "What's the good news, Coach?" He said, "The good news is that if he can get a girl in his room, any of y'all can." I said, "How did you know they were going to ask for the bad news first?" He said, "They always ask for the bad news first."

Coach Erk Russell

FIT HAPPENS

Lynn Hughes

Hughes, 63, played and coached for the Georgia Bulldogs. He lives in Marietta, Georgia.

I went to Georgia in '62, redshirted in '63, and played in '64, '65 and '66 for Dooley. He was a very intense person. That first off-season program we went through was the worst I'd ever seen. The workouts were grueling—a lot of running, a lot of exercising, a lot of drills, a lot of weights. It was tough, and then spring practice was brutal.

In 1966, Kirby Moore, our starting quarterback, got hurt in the Kentucky game right after halftime. Kentucky had driven the ball down to about our two-yard line and fumbled. They were leading. Coach Dooley said to me, "We're going to put you in. You know what to do." Our offense wasn't very complicated in those days. I started to run onto the field, and Coach Erk Russell, the head defensive coordinator, hollered, "Little Lennie," he used to call me that. He walked out and puts his arm around my shoulder. I loved this guy—everybody loved Erk Russell. I thought he was going to give me words of encouragement. I should have known better. Coach Russell looked at me and said, "Little Lennie, you ain't much, but you're all we got."

The first game I started was in Tuscaloosa, Alabama. It was Coach Dooley's first game against Alabama. The opposing quarterback was a guy named **JOE WILLIE NAMATH**[*]. This was before he hurt his knees. Do you think he could throw the ball well? Well, he could run the ball better than he could throw it! We got beat 31-3.

[*]To make sure that JOE NAMATH attended Alabama his freshman year, Alabama Assistant Coach Howard Schnellenberger drove to Beaver Falls, Pennsylvania, picked up Namath and drove him to Tuscaloosa.

My first year playing defense was '65. Steve Spurrier and I got to know each other that year. During the Georgia-Florida game, a fight broke out when Florida was on offense. Steve just stood there leaning on my shoulder pads. He and I were talking to each other and watching the fight. It was a funny picture.

Playing and coaching Georgia football opened up many business opportunities for me throughout the state. So many people I have known in business through the years were in school with me. Both U.S. senators from the state are good friends from college. Johnny Isakson lived next to me in the dorm the first year I was there. Saxby Chambliss and I were in business school together. The governor played at Georgia. Anywhere I go, if I want to find out

> Coach Russell looked at me and said, "Little Lennie, you ain't much, but you're all we got."

something, I generally know somebody to call, or I can call on somebody who knows who I am and will give me the opportunity to sit down and talk. I got a great education, which I would never have been able to get had I not been on scholarship there. I met a lot of great people and made a lot of great friends. You create a special bond with the guys you play with. We had a party for the championship team of '66. It was great to go back and see all of them and see what they're doing now.

SOMETIMES GOD JUST HANDS YOU ONE

Claude McBride

*McBride, 77, lives in Athens Georgia. He grad-
uated from Georgia in '53. He is retired but
still serves as an associate in the alumni office.
He was team chaplain from 1969 until 2002,
when Coach Richt decided he wanted a full
time chaplain, and McBride was not available. Today he serves as chaplain for the
Fellowship of Christian Athletes.*

When I came to Athens as a pastor of Miller Avenue Baptist Church, it occurred to me that the first group of
students to arrive at UGA were the freshmen football
players. They brought them in early, even before the varsity players came on campus. I got to thinking about how they recruit
these guys, and then all of a sudden the boys show up, and
they're alone on this big campus. I wrote to
all of them and congratulated them on
having been selected for their scholarship
and for wearing the Georgia Red and Black
and invited them to come to church on
Sunday, telling them they would be welcome. I encouraged them to at least go to
their church. Some showed up.

> When the wrecker was jacking the car up, a bible fell out.

After the first Sunday when some boys had shown up, I got a
late-night call from a wrecker driver. He said there had been a
terrible accident on the highway leaving Athens. Two people
were killed. A couple of guys running from the police had run a
stop sign and ran into the Yawn family, who had just brought
their son, Bruce, a freshman football player, up for school. The
family had come to church that morning. When the wrecker was
jacking the car up, a bible fell out. There was a program from our

church from the morning service with my name and number on it. So the tow truck driver called me. He told me he was thinking of that kid there by himself, and they didn't know if his mother was going to live, and his father was in real bad shape. The whole family is just in a terrible mess. I thanked him and said I would get right out there.

I rushed to the hospital, about ten o'clock at night. When I walked into the waiting room, there was Coach Dooley and Erk Russell, the defensive coach, and all the freshman players. They had heard about the accident and had come to the hospital to be with Bruce. When I walked in the emergency room door, Bruce recognized me. He came over and hugged me. The coaches were thinking, "Well, who is that?" There hadn't been time for anybody from Statesboro, where he was from, to get there. That was my beginning. His family was all right. His mother had a tough time, including several operations, but, thankfully, she recovered.

Bruce continued to come to church and bring others with him. Soon we had a large group and they asked me to be the pastor/advisor for their FCA chapter. It grew from that. One day Vince Dooley was speaking at the Kiwanis Club and said to me, "Coach Russell mentioned to me that we should make you chaplain of the football team because so many of the guys go out to your church." He asked me to write down what I thought being team chaplain would involve, because there were no other programs that we knew of in '69. I wrote down what I thought a chaplain should do and gave the information, including the idea that it should be a voluntary position, to him. The next week his secretary called and asked me if I could come by the next day.

When I went to Coach Dooley's office, he said, "I read what you wrote." We discussed it for a minute, and he said, "Whoops. We'd better get on downstairs." I went with him, and he introduced me as the official team chaplain. That was the first I knew about it. I traveled with the team to games, including bowl games. I ate with them a good bit at their dorm. I did a lot of individual counseling, weddings and, unfortunately, some funerals. It was the beginning of a fantastic relationship.

UPON FURTHER REVIEW

Coach Dooley and I became friends after my playing days. I had a tremendous amount of respect for him. He was not somebody that most players, early on, got close to. He was not much older than we were. He was only 34 at that time. One of the most interesting things about Coach Dooley was that he always knew what was going to come out when he opened his mouth. Regardless of the situation in a game, he knew what he was going to do. I don't think he ever second-guessed his decisions. So many coaches react to outside pressure, but he never did. He had a game plan. He allowed his assistant coaches to coach, but I think all the players knew who the boss was, and the assistants did, too. He's one of the best organizers and team leaders I've ever known in that respect.

—BRUCE YAWN, player '65-'68, Statesboro, GA

I've met Coach Dooley a number of times. When I was in law school, I had five Georgia football players in my law school class. I told Coach Dooley that when we met at a function. He said he had only had 25 players go through law school in his entire career. Interestingly, five of them were in the graduating class of 1970.

—GREG GRIFFIN, Georgia Class of '72

Erk Russell, assistant head coach and defensive coordinator for the Georgia Bulldogs, was later athletic director at Georgia Southern. I needed some information and ran into Coach Russell after he had moved to Statesboro. I said, "Coach, I use a lot of sports analogies when I do management seminars. Can you give me one on motivation since you are the best motivator I have ever met?" He said, "Motivation is taking a fellow and getting him to reach down inside himself and grab a hold of something he didn't know was there." I thought that was one of the great comments I've ever heard on motivation.

—LEN DAVIS, 64, Athens, Ga.

The only coach I've known well is the legendary coach, William Hartman, Jr. Bill Hartman pioneered the Notre Dame box formation and the jump pass at the University of Georgia as an assistant coach. He had a twinkle in his eye, great good humor and never said anything ill of anyone. He's right there with Dan Magill in terms of having one of the best memories for sports minutiae of anyone I have ever met. Coach Hartman's son, also named Bill, is a sports broadcaster. He was having breakfast with a group of us one morning. I said, "I am astonished at your father's memory. He has a mind like a trap. He remembers everything." He said, "Len, that may be. But, it may also be that anyone who could challenge his memory is dead now."

—LEN DAVIS, 64, Athens, Georgia

Coach Dooley was very quiet and calm. He was a great leader. It was Coach Dooley who said, "If you don't do the work during the week, you're certainly not going to be prepared to win the game on Saturday." He always had his teams prepared.

> I remember asking Erk...if he made it look that way and had a pre-cut on his head like the wrestlers did.

I thought the world of Coach Dooley. I think the world of Coach Richt. When Coach Richt signed with Georgia, his very first speech was to the Macon Touchdown Club. I had purchased a Bible that I wanted Coach Richt to autograph for my mother, who is 85 years old and lives in Cordele, Georgia. She's one of the biggest Bulldog fans I've ever known. When I went up to his table that night, everybody was getting helmets, footballs and pennants autographed. I pulled out that Bible, and he seemed to be heart-warmed by the sight of it. Coach Richt is such a fine Christian man. He went on a mission trip to Honduras recently. He leads by example, and he lives what he preaches. Georgia has been so fortunate.

—FRANKLIN S. HORNE, JR., attorney, Macon

Erk Russell is famous for head-butting his players with his bald head on their helmets. He was trying to draw blood from his head, so he could storm up and down the sidelines throughout the game with this little trickle of blood coming down. He wanted to get the crowd fired up and get his players fired up like he was leading them in to battle, and he was going to take the first hit. I remember asking Erk one time, in kind of a funny way, if he really popped that guy on the helmet full force, or if he made it look that way and had a pre-cut on his head like the wrestlers did. Russell just gave a little smile and a wink. Now, I'm putting words in his mouth because all he did was give me that Cheshire-cat grin, but it was almost like he said, "I'm not really going to hurt myself by hitting a 260-pound guy on his hard helmet as hard as I can with my head, but I'm going to make sure everybody sees me do it." Erk also came up with the "Junkyard Dawgs" for his defense in the mid 1970s. James Brown was a semi-mascot for Georgia then and he ended up writing a song about it. For four or five home games, we had James Brown on the sidelines with the cheerleaders singing, "Junkyard Dawgs," to the crowd, getting them fired up. Erk liked to take credit for coming up with that catch phrase.

—RICK FRANZMAN, UGA '75

I lived in Athens a couple of years when I was a teenager. I made friends with a Georgia player from Pennsylvania. This would have been 1950 or '51. He was dating a girl who lived in our apartment house. We thought he was something. He said, "Well, you boys just come down to the Memorial Hall, and I'll take you in to the game." We got to go to every home game for free. The players used to dress outside the stadium. Then they would walk in and we'd walk with them straight onto the field. It was something being there with the players and coaches. They told us to stay out of the way. We were just there having a great time on the sidelines. That was when Wally Butts was the coach. They didn't have great teams in those years, but they were tough. I used to watch them in practice. Man alive, you talk about learning some language. I learned some language. I remember thinking if I ever got a chance to play football, "I ain't coming over here. It's too mean."

I remember Ed Thilenius calling the games. He wasn't Munson, of course, but he was probably, to me, the second best announcer we've ever had. He was a Bulldog all the way.

Two or three years ago, my son and I went to a Bulldog meeting. They had a private room. Dooley and Coach Richt were standing inside. I had met Coach Richt before, and he remembered me from the Motor Coach Club—we donate about $10,000 every year to his fund. We got to talk to them for about 30 minutes. We were in heaven. Coach Richt is so down-to-earth. It was fantastic to be able to talk to him. He said, "We built new locker rooms and hallways with your donations." He was very, very appreciative. Loren Smith introduced him at his first meeting. He said, "We have got the right man." He said that before he had ever coached a game. He knew exactly what he was talking about. That has been proven true.

Georgia football is a part of my life. I spend very little time fishing anymore. I can't wait for football season. I plan my life around Georgia football. I'm 71 years old. I make dang sure, if I work it right, I can handle getting to every game. I probably spent too much money on hunting and fishing. Now I spend my entertainment money on Georgia. I've had my season tickets since the seventies, maybe longer than that—40 years at least.

—**FRANK SAXON**, Athens High, Class of '54

I graduated from Georgia in 1965, which was Vince Dooley's first year. That was an exciting time to be at Georgia. When I was in school, the campus was dry, but it was very open, especially during the Georgia-Florida game. It was a different time—an innocent time. My sophomore year, 1962, we were 3-3-4. The games were so boring we took our programs and made paper airplanes. Everybody threw paper airplanes around the stadium—thousands and thousands of paper airplanes flew all over the place. When Vince came, we had this new enthusiasm. He redid the uniforms and put the "G" on the helmet. He came out with this new silver and red. We wound up winning seven out of ten and went on to beat **TEXAS TECH*** in the Sun Bowl. Man, we were excited.

The next year, we beat Alabama in an upset with a flea-flicker, and then went up to Michigan. We beat them with a field goal. We won the next two or three games, and we were ranked fifth in the country. We hadn't been ranked fifth since 1940.

> *Former Indiana basketball coach Bobby Knight later became the coach of the Red Raiders of TEXAS TECH. Tech's basketball arena, The Spirit Center, is on Indiana Avenue. The nickname of Knight's high school in Orrville, Ohio is the Red Raiders.

> ## We ran into Coach Russell on Bourbon Street. He had this big cigar.

I love Erk Russell. He's a great character. I was at New Orleans when we won the national championship. We ran into Coach Russell on Bourbon Street. He had this big cigar. A real pretty girl came up to him and said, "I'm Penny. We just think you're wonderful." He said, "I think you're wonderful, too, sweetheart." And then he walked on.

—**NEELY YOUNG**, 66, Marietta, Georgia

Coach Dooley was a great organizer, a great administrator. Nothing ever surprised him. He was prepared for every possible contingency. He rarely showed emotion. My junior year, we played the University of Houston in Athens. They had a running back named Paul Gibson, and a fullback, Carlos Bell, who were unbelievable. They had beaten us to death. The score was only 10-7, but they had already rushed for 400+ yards. Yet, we were hanging in there because they would go up and down the field, and every time they would get inside the 10-yard line, they would fumble the ball. We had an opportunity at the very end to tie the game. Coach Dooley grabbed our field goal kicker, Jim McCullough, at the top of the shoulder pads like he was going to wring his neck, and he started shaking him. Coach Dooley was red-faced and acting totally out of character. He said, "You've been on scholarship here for three years. You get your rear end in there, and you earn that scholarship and make this kick." I almost fainted right there on the sidelines! That emotion was so out of character, it was unbelievable. He made the kick and we tied Houston 10-10.

Coach Dooley and I are like father and son. He and I are as close or closer than any of his former players. He has been such a mentor to me. He was one of the early people I went to when I had the Olympics idea. He's one of the few who didn't laugh at me. He said, "What can I do to help?" He was a great help in the strategy early on and in the execution that the University of Georgia was such an important part of. He helped me sit down and analyze. As you begin to bid for the Games, you have to seek out people who are experts in all the various sports that are part of the Olympic program. He helped me identify those people in our area who would be a great resource to me. He offered whole-heartedly the resources of the University of Georgia and the athletic department. They did such a fabulous job with the women's soccer. He was there for me in all the tough moments. It was a hard job. Every now and then, I needed a shoulder to cry on. His was it.

Barbara Dooley and my wife are great friends. We've had a wonderful relationship with them forever. We have admired and been amazed at her energy level. She has boundless energy and passion.

It would be very difficult for me to overemphasize the contributions that Vince Dooley has made to the University of Georgia. They are almost beyond measure in terms of the quality of the competitive athletic programs. He is the guy who is responsible for all that.

—BILLY PAYNE, 60, Atlanta, GA

There was a time when Vince Dooley was thinking about leaving Georgia and going back to Auburn. At the same time, there was a song about Tom Dooley, "Hang Down Your Head, Tom Dooley." Somebody changed the words around to make the song about Vince Dooley and not going back to Auburn. He had all of us on pins and needles when he was trying to make that decision but fortunately for us, he decided to stay.

—STEVE STANCIL, Canton, GA

The football team flew to Kentucky in 1974. They held everybody on the plane because somebody had written on the window that there was a bomb on the airplane. We had to stand out on the tarmac until the authorities came to talk to all of us. They told us that they knew it was a lineman who did it because 'airplane' was spelled wrong.

> ...they knew it was a lineman who did it because 'airplane' was spelled wrong.

—CRAIG HERTWIG, Offensive Tackle, Captain, '74

Vince Dooley, who is the closest thing we have to a deity in Georgia football lore, is a graduate of Auburn and was an assistant football coach there before he came to Georgia. I also, quite frankly, root for Auburn every week except for when they're playing Georgia because, again, it's a big rivalry to a lot of people in our school. I would be delighted for Georgia and Auburn to be undefeated every year when they went into their game.

One year, I was so confident Auburn was going to clean our clock, I went to a continuing education seminar in Yosemite National Park and skipped the game altogether, which is really rare for me. I called my wife during a break in the seminar, and she gave me the halftime score. Georgia was way ahead. I thought she was pulling my leg. Fortunately, she wasn't. Some good friends recorded the game for me so I could watch it when I got home.

> Pat Dye was as tough as anybody you've ever seen.

Vince Dooley grew up in Mobile. When I lived in Mobile, in the mid-eighties, I was a member of the L.A. Georgia Bulldog Club—the 'Lower Alabama' Bulldog Club. Vince came home to visit family, and we had a party and reception in his honor. I cannot think of a finer human being to represent a university. What a gracious man, a true, true gentleman. I went through the receiving line and shook his hand and told him, "Coach, I was in school when we won the national championship in 1980—that's a once-in-a-lifetime experience." He said, "No, it wasn't. Don't ever say that. It was not an once-in-a-lifetime experience. It will happen again." He was nice about it, but he was also very clear. He didn't want me using that kind of language when I was talking about a national championship.

—MARK KING, UGA '82, Dalton, Georgia, native

I was the first coach hired by Vince Dooley when he went to the University of Georgia. Sometimes Coach Dooley and I would go into people's homes recruiting. Often the first thing he'd do is look at the student and ask, "Son, what are you interested in studying?" The first time he did that, I said to myself, "Oh, my gosh. We probably lost that person because that kid isn't interested in doing anything but playing football." I told Coach, "Ask about his grandmother and his granddad and his girlfriends from now on." We recruited primarily in Georgia, Florida and the Southeast. We had to get to know the girlfriends and their granddaddies and whether they liked to go fishing and what their other interests were.

Erk Russell and I recruited many times together. He was always very cheerful. He always had a little cigar smoked right down to the nub, hanging out of his mouth. We all loved him. He was a great fellow to be around.

Pat Dye was as tough as anybody you've ever seen. He's from a little town near Augusta—he and his two brothers. They say they walked eight miles to practice every day and back. Pat Dye played on the South All-Stars the year I coached the North All-Stars. Fran Tarkenton was my quarterback. Pat played guard, and you just couldn't run against him. He was all over the field. He was a real competitor.

> That spring practice was tougher than any boot camp that's ever been.

It was tough to be in Coach Butts' camps. We went through the longest spring practice in the history of football when we came back from World War II. We started in January and didn't have the spring game that year until some time in May. That spring practice was tougher than any boot camp that's ever been. I don't remember ever having any water during those practices. I just remember everybody hollering at us that we'd better be doing our jobs. All of Coach Butts' players had a little bit of fear of him, but, after I started coaching over there, I got to know him real well. We'd go have coffee together. Coach Butts had a lot of warmth to him and he had a big heart. He was ferocious and a hard-nosed coach, but after I got to know him, I had a totally different picture.

—HOWARD "DOC" AYERS, Assistant Coach UGA '64-'80,
Retired, Cedartown, Georgia

I knew Coach Russell very well. The 1974 season had not been too good. A lot of people were criticizing the coaching staff. We happened to be at Coach Russell's house after a game—we had lost to Vanderbilt. Coach Russell wanted to talk about his defense. He had a knack for giving every player a nickname. He made the statement, "I wonder what I could come up with for a name for the defense." I suggested "Junkyard Dawgs." Erk liked that so much, he took it and started off the season with the defense being named the "Junkyard Dawgs," which still is carried forward today.

Coach Goff is a very upbeat guy. He really didn't like all the limelight that went along with the job when he was coaching, but his personality is such that he befriends a lot of people. There was a split in the Georgia supporters when he got fired. About 50 percent didn't want him and 50 percent did. He has turned out to be a very astute businessman and has done extremely well since leaving his coaching job. He never said one unkind thing about Georgia.

—JIMMY MATTHEWS, Albany, Georgia,
season ticket holder since 1965

Coach Dooley was at a practice. He came up to me hollering at me about moving my feet. He started pounding his fist into my chest and telling me how I had to be moving my feet the way he was pounding. To me, that was pretty funny, but I certainly couldn't have laughed at the time.

—CRAIG HERTWIG, former lineman, Athens, GA

Since I graduated, my wife and I are involved in different civic and church organizations. We've met Vince Dooley several times at different places. He is the chair of one of our organizations. I'm a CPA and work for myself. I have a client called Southern Catholic College, and they built a new college up in Dawsonville, Georgia. Vince Dooley is Catholic and he's involved with their golf tournament every year. He's always been the chairperson for this golf tournament. I've been working there with them, off and on, for about seven years now.

The first time we approached him to come help out Southern Catholic, we went to Vince's house. Growing up in Athens, I always knew where Vince Dooley's house was, but I never went into his house. We were actually meeting with Barbara Dooley because we wanted her to be on the board of directors of the college. We wanted Vince to be involved with the fundraising. We went there right after lunch and met with Barbara Dooley. Right as we walked in....The house itself is nice and everything...but nothing could compare to this seating area where on the walls all of these "coach of the year" awards were for Vince. They had names of **BEAR BRYANT***, Johnny Majors and had Vince Dooley up there and it made it surreal. Just to see all the different pictures with each team and football trophies. It was an NCAA memorabilia Mecca.

It put it all in perspective as to what he accomplished. The best part of that was that up on the fireplace over the mantle was a picture of Herschel Walker going for a touchdown against Notre Dame. The guy I was with, who was founder of Southern Catholic College, is a Notre Dame graduate. I was pointing at that picture going, "Yeah. Do you remember that? Remember that?" It was funny to rub that into him. That was quite an experience inside the house.

I would describe Vince Dooley as very humble, really humble, just his personality, very approachable. I didn't have any problem asking him questions. At the last golf tournament he was at, he came around to all the golfers, individually. When he rolled up, it was right after a Tennessee game where Georgia fell apart in the second half. I believe it was 55-37. He barely gets out of his golf cart, and I said, "Coach, what would you have done different? What happened?" He had no problem giving some of his coach comments. He's very approachable and didn't have any problems talking with anybody. He's just a good man.

—_GREG ERBS_, 39, CPA, Cummings, GA

Several years ago Ray Goff was contacted by the Jacksonville Sports and Entertainment Board and notified that he was going to be inducted into the Georgia-Florida Hall of Fame. The Georgia-Florida Hall of Fame celebrates the annual Georgia-Florida football game and the great rivalry between the two universities. He was asked if he could participate in the induction ceremonies. Coach Goff said he would be honored to come but he had just one question. "What was that?" they asked. "Who's inducting me, Georgia or Florida?"

When Mark Richt first came to the University of Georgia, Dicky Clark, a former player at Georgia and head of the Fellowship of

*In the TV show "B.J. and the Bear," Bear was a chimpanzee named after **BEAR BRYANT**.

Christian

Christian Athletes, got together with Coach Richt and one of the things that was on their agenda was the need for a full-time chaplain for the football team. They had discussed this need and, with Coach Richt's encouragement, Dicky contacted Dr. James Merritt, a true died-in-the wool Georgia Bulldog fan. James, an old friend, called me and told me that we needed to help Coach Richt find a chaplain for the football team. We called around to some of the guys we knew and set up a luncheon at the little clubhouse I have on my farm. We met on a Saturday at noon and Coach Richt came to the meeting. That was the first time I had met Mark Richt and I was very impressed. Anyway, Mark spoke to the group, and Dicky spoke to the group and we discussed the need to put together a program to get a full-time chaplain. Out of that Saturday lunch meeting on my farm evolved a program that brought current team chaplain Kevin "Chappy" Hynes to the Bulldogs and formed Team United under the auspices of the Fellowship of Christian Athletes. I was very impressed by his concern for his players' academic, athletic and, with this action, spiritual welfare....

> I was very impressed by his concern for his players' academic, athletic and... spiritual welfare.

While still in Tallahassee, during a Sunday school class, Mark and his wife Katharyn participated in a discussion over whose responsibility orphans were. The conclusion of the discussion was that they are the responsibility of all of us. Mark and Katharyn discussed the issue further between themselves and decided that they wanted to be proactive about it. Katharyn went to the Ukraine for several weeks to search for a child to adopt and begin the adoption process. Mark followed her to the Ukraine later. My understanding is that the process begins with the prospective adoptive parents stating up front how many children they want and whether they want boys or girls. Once they make their decision they are bound to it. They then go through a process of determining whether they are suitable adoptive parents. The Richts had decided that they wanted a little boy. They then went through the paperwork and interviews to get a little boy they would bring home and raise and love as their own. They were determined to complete the process and fulfill their obligation as Christian parents. While they were going through the process to adopt a little boy, Katharyn found this little girl who was also an orphan and was also a disfigured child. Katharyn had noticed that there were people across the street from the orphanage and she was told that they were waiting to take the orphans who reached the age of twelve and were not adopted. These people seemed to be somewhat shady and it was Katharyn's opinion that their intentions were just not good. She had inquired about the fate of the little disfigured girl and was told that her future was questionable and probably bleak. Katharyn then asked the authorities if she could have her too. The authorities, somewhat surprised, agreed that this was probably the best hope for the little girl, and allowed the Richts to adopt the little girl too. So Mark and Katharyn flew back to the United States with their two new children, Anya and Zack. After long hours in the air and the rigors of travel they were met at home by their two young boys, Jonathan and David. Jonathan and David quickly introduced their new brother and sister to the family with a dip in the family pool. They are now a very happy family. This story is just a small part of why we are so lucky to have such a wonderful man and his family as members of the family of the University of Georgia.

—**ARCHIE B. CRENSHAW**, 72, Oconee County

The margin of error in a college football poll is plus or minus 100%

Chapter 5

Put Me in Coach

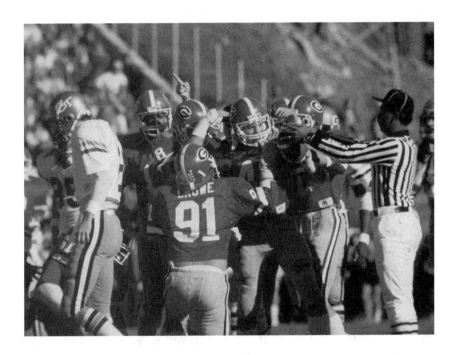

Bulldog Heroes, Like Bulldog Memories, Never Grow Old

HE WASN'T ALWAYS A SAINT

Jon Stinchcomb

Jon Stinchcomb, 28, of Lilburn, Georgia, followed his brother Matthew, captain of the '98 Bulldogs, to Georgia. Stinchcomb now plays for the New Orleans Saints.

M ost of the SEC and ACC schools were recruiting me, including Florida State, Tennessee, Auburn, Florida, Clemson, and, also Texas, **NEBRASKA***, and Colorado. It was important for me to play in my home state. My brother played at the University of Georgia. Although I looked at other schools, I always compared them to the University of Georgia.

I wanted to go to a good school. Academics were important to me. I wanted to play for a competitive football team. I wanted to feel comfortable on campus. I wanted to stay within a reasonable distance of my family. The coach most active in recruiting me was Chris Scelfo under Jim Donnan.

Coach Scelfo became almost a friend during the recruiting process. In hindsight, I don't know how great an idea it was, considering six months later he was my college coach, and I was under his tutelage. The relationship changed, which is, I guess, to be expected, but I was young and naive. During the recruiting process, you feel like you're the golden child, like the program might fall apart if you don't go there. After the first snap, you realize you've got a long way to go. I was playing guard across from Richard Seymour. By the end of the play, I was looking at the top of the stadium, because I was firmly planted on my hind-part. It was a quick awakening for me.

> *Academic All-American teams have been picked every year since 1952. NEBRASKA leads all colleges by a wide margin in number of players selected.

My senior year in high school, **NATE HYBL*** and I came early to the University of Georgia. Right before our first day of class, we got a knock on the door. We were thinking we're pretty cool—right? We already had friends! We were greeted by a trash can full of water. We spent the rest of the night using shirts and towels to push the water out of our room. That was our welcoming present.

I went to Georgia football games with my brother when he was being recruited. We stood in the end zone, where we could see Garrison Hearst running 60-yard touchdown runs. I remember some of Eric Zeier's throws. As a kid, I thought he threw it a mile! Later, when I played, I thought, "Golly, those are the same guys I looked up to for so many years."

The first time I ran out on the field at Sanford Stadium as a player, it felt like a rite of passage, almost a fulfillment of a dream. When you set your goal, or when you get close to accomplishing a goal, you move a little further back. What I mean is that in high school, I wanted to play football in college. Then I wanted to play for a big program. Once I got to Athens, being on the field was important. Then, I wanted to be a starter. Once I become a starter, I wanted to be one of the best on the team. I'm always striving for more.

My memories of Georgia football go back to the guys on the team. We had guys like Curt McGill who was a comedian and Brady Pate, quick with a joke. It's more the guys I remember than the actual stories.

I went back recently to Sanford Stadium for the Mississippi State game. It felt different to go as a fan. As I get older, I know fewer and fewer guys there. As a player in the NFL, I can hardly enjoy a game without trying to break down what the defense did and what plays it looked like they were about to run. It's much more tactical than actually appreciating it for what it is—an enjoyable football game to watch.

***NATE HYBL** is the only athlete in the history of collegiate sports to win a national title in two different sports at two different schools: Golf at Georgia and Football at Oklahoma.

Playing in the Georgia-Florida game was a unique experience. Most other games were either home games with everybody cheering for us, or an away game where they were booing us—and we were the worst team to come down their path. The Georgia-Florida game in Jacksonville was a great atmosphere. I hated that I was blanked my whole career in the Florida game. I still have fond memories of it—not many, but some, like the bus ride from the hotel. We weren't in Athens, but the streets were lined for miles with fans. They were holding up signs and chanting and waving their little pom pon shakers at the bus.

> LSU fans were tough....little kids flipping the bird, and older women saying things that almost made me blush.

LSU fans were tough. They stick out in my mind since now I'm in New Orleans. There were little kids flipping the bird and older women saying things that almost made me blush. At the stadium when you looked around, you couldn't see anything else. There were no tall buildings in the horizon. It felt like we were playing in the middle of nowhere. It was a wild place. The LSU fans were shaking our bus. It was hard for us to get through with them beating their flags against the bus windows. If you play for LSU, it's to your advantage—you've got some rabid fans. I'm sure the same people who wear the purple and gold are wearing the black and gold of the Saints on Sundays for me.

The fans at Sanford are great, especially when we started the 'Dawg Walk.' We didn't do that my entire career. It's a personal interaction with the fans on the way to the stadium. We'd get our high right before the game.

I try not to have any game-day superstitions, because if you don't do it, you feel like you've already jinxed yourself. I try not to have any habits or superstitions...so, that's my superstition—not having any.

After my senior year, Uga and I were scheduled to be in the Savannah St. Patrick's Day parade. We were going to ride on the same flatbed. As we were going through the parade, it became painfully

NORTH SIDE

AISLE

ROW

SEAT

DEDICATION

SANFORD STADIUM FIELD

UNIVERSITY OF GEORGIA

YALE

VERSUS

GEORGIA

Old College 1801

Connecticut Hall 1752

SATURDAY, OCTOBER 12, 1929
KICK-OFF 2 P.M. EASTERN TIME
PRICE $3.00

HOLD YOUR OWN TICKET

YALE

There are some who say you can marry a Georgia Tech fan, yet still go on to lead a normal and productive life.

Sports Illustrated

September 11, 1967

40 CE

COLLEGE FOOTBALL

GEORGIA

NOTRE DAME

THE
FIGHT
FOR
No. 1

TEXAS

MIAMI

Sports Illustrated

October 13, 1969   50 CENTS

THE WILD SOUTHEAST

Georgia's Bruce Kemp Overruns South Carolina

Sports Illustrated

November 17, 1980

NOW GEORGIA IS NO.1

Freshman Sensati
Herschel Walk

Credit: Andy Hayt/Sports Illustrated/Getty Images

0 10094

46

724454

Sports Illustrated

August 31, 1981

AUGUST 31, 1981 $1.75

TOP DAWG
Herschel Walker of Georgia,
a Profile by Curry Kirkpatrick

TOP FROGS
A Memoir of TCU's Glory Days
by Dan Jenkins (who's biased)

TOP CONFERENCE
It's the Pac-10,
says John Papanek

TOP 20

1. Michigan	11. Georgia
2. Texas	12. Pittsburgh
3. USC	13. Florida
4. Oklahoma	14. Ohio State
5. Notre Dame	15. Washington
6. Penn State	16. Miss. State
7. Nebraska	17. Stanford
8. Alabama	18. BYU
9. UCLA	19. LSU
10. N. Carolina	20. Baylor

724454

35

Sports Illustrated

March 1, 1982

WILL HERSCHEL WALKER TURN PRO NOW?

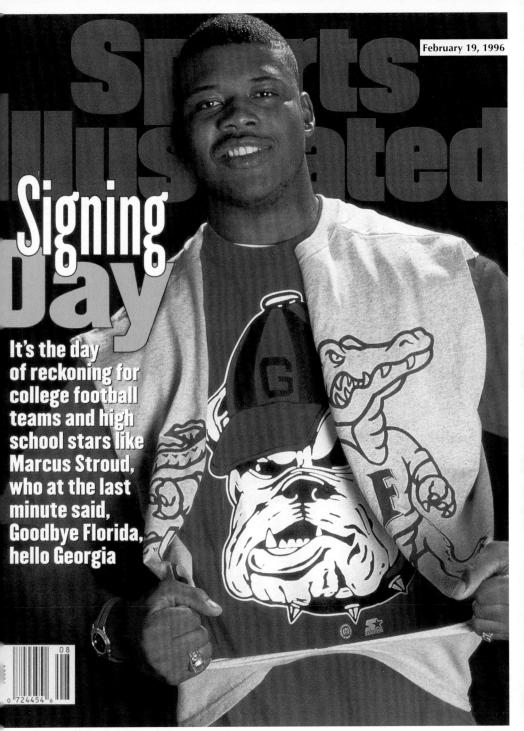

February 19, 1996

Sports Illustrated

Signing Day

It's the day
of reckoning for
college football
teams and high
school stars like
Marcus Stroud,
who at the last
minute said,
Goodbye Florida,
hello Georgia

08

0 724454 6

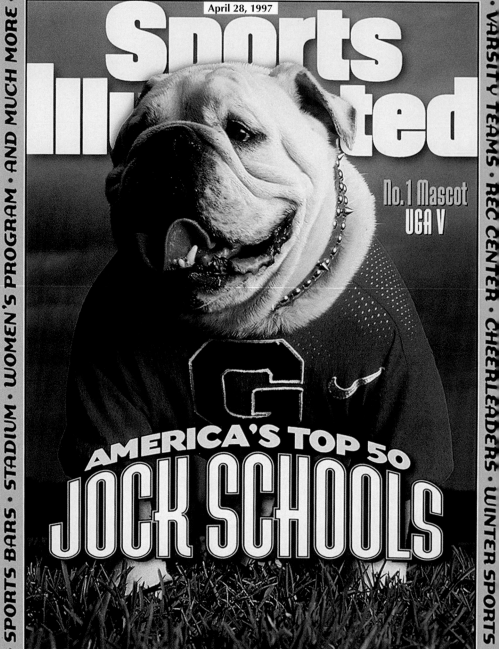

WHO'S GOT THE BEST INTRAMURALS · FIGHT SONG

April 28, 1997

Sports Illustrated

VARSITY TEAMS · REC CENTER · CHEERLEADERS · WINTER SPORTS

AND MUCH MORE · WOMEN'S PROGRAM · STADIUM · SPORTS BARS

No. 1 Mascot
UGA V

AMERICA'S TOP 50
JOCK SCHOOLS

PEP RALLIES · TAILGATING · PICKUP BASKETBALL

COLLEGE FOOTBALL

2004 PREVIEW

August 16, 2004

Sports Illustrated

SI's TOP

10

Jason
White
Oklahoma

David
Greene
Georgia

Skyler
Green
LSU

Frank
Gore
Miami

1. USC
2. Oklahoma
3. LSU
4. Georgia
5. Miami
6. Florida
7. Texas
8. Ohio State
9. Florida St.
10. Kansas St.

Matt
Leinart
USC

PLUS
Complete
Scouting Reports
117 Teams Ranked

$3.99US $4.99CAN

33

0 70989 10241 5

2008 COLLEGE FOOTBALL

PREVIEW

Sports Illustrated

www.SI.com

AUGUST 11, 2008

No. 1 GEORGIA

Who Will Challenge the Dawgs?

34 PAGES OF SCOUTING REPORTS

SI Ranks All 119 Teams

SI's Top 10 ▷

No. 2 OHIO STATE
LB James Laurinaitis QB Todd Boeckman RB Chris Wells

No. 3 USC
LB Brian Cushing QB Mark Sanchez LB Rey Maualuga

No. 4 MISSOURI
LB Sean Weatherspoon WR Jeremy Maclin

No. 5 FLORIDA
LB Brandon Spikes QB Tim Tebow WR Percy Harvin

No. 6 OKLAHOMA   No. 7 AUBURN
No. 8 TEXAS TECH   No. 9 LSU   No. 10 WISCONSIN

CONFERENCE PROJECTIONS P.100

THE SPREAD OFFENSE
How It Works • How to Stop It

With
Bonus Gatefold P. 55

LB DANNELL ELLERBE   QB MATTHEW STAFFORD   RB KNOWSHON MORENO obvious that people couldn't care less that I was on the float. They just loved Uga. They asked, "Are you his handler?" I thought, "I am now, I guess!!!" There was a sign on the side of the float saying who I was...but, they really couldn't care less. All they wanted was to be with the dog. It was very humbling.

> ...Uga and I were scheduled to be in the Savannah St. Patrick's Day parade.

Without a doubt, as an NFL player, there's a bond with other Georgia players. We have a school pride in the locker room. When I play other NFL teams, I always scan the roster looking for Georgia guys. That's fun. It doesn't matter if I played with the guys, or if they're a little older. I never played with Philip Daniels, but after the Washington Redskin game, we were shooting the breeze. It's definitely a fraternity-type deal. There's a pride that comes with being a Georgia Bulldog.

NFL players are a roomful of guys who have that same school pride with their schools. We used to have three Auburn players in our locker room, Victor Riley, Wayne Gandy and Willy Whitehead, so it was pretty brutal when we lost to them. We've got a couple of guys from **OHIO STATE***, and we haven't played them but they're always wearing their Buckeye gear and they're pretty noisy.

Georgia football, for me, was a life-changing experience. It's been a part of my life since I was a kid. It's offered opportunities that I would otherwise not even have come close to. I am forever indebted to the impact it has had on my life. It comes with a lot of pride and a lot of history, and when you get that, you want to be a part of it.

---

*In the 1976 OHIO STATE-Indiana game, the Hoosiers scored on the first play of the second quarter. Indiana coach, Lee Corso, called a timeout. During the timeout, Corso had his team pose for a group picture with the scoreboard—showing Indiana leading Ohio State 7-6—clearly visible in the background. Corso featured the picture on the cover of the 1977 Indiana recruiting brochure. Ohio State won the game 47-7.

BUTTS BARED

Tom Lewis

Tom Lewis, 69, lives in Alpharetta, Georgia, and is an Assistant Chief Pilot for AirTran. He played quarterback for Georgia in 1957-1959, when playing was just a little different than it is today.

There were a lot of factors in my going to Georgia. Being my home state university had a lot to do with it. Coach Wally Butts had been at Georgia for many years, but it didn't seem like they were getting the good football players. I chose to go there, thinking we could turn things around. Coach Butts' reputation and the fact that it was the University of Georgia made me very happy to go to Athens.

> He would nearly die if he thought we were going to get a drink of water.

Coach Butts was a determined, dynamic, harsh individual. Yet, we could tell deep down inside he had a heart of gold. He really cared about his players; although, we never knew it out there on the field, especially in practice. Back in those days, there was no such thing as heat, no such thing as water, no such thing as rest. He would nearly die if he thought we were going to get a drink of water. Nowadays, they take breaks every 15 minutes and fill up with fluids. We could never do that. He pushed us from the time we got on the field till the time we got off, but we respected him. We knew that he was doing the best he could for us, and we did the same for him. I wouldn't say it was from fear; although, a lot of guys did fear him. I never feared him, but I always respected him.

In '59, my senior year, we started off playing Alabama with Coach Bear Bryant, and we beat them. Then, we moved ahead from there. We could see the pride Coach Butts was building up in our team and in himself as we progressed and got better each week. The best thing about him was that we could see him really, really get excited about what was going on—excited about the team and excited about the players and excited about our success. It meant so much to us because there had been many years that we weren't successful. That year we won the Southeastern Conference and played in the **ORANGE BOWL*** on January 1, 1960. To be able to bring back the glory to the University of Georgia that they had known in earlier years was the best thing.

Fran Tarkenton was a class below me. Fran was a good college quarterback, an All-American. In college he didn't have the speed or the arm that you look for in an All-Pro or Hall-of-Famer, although he did the best with what he had. The thing that made Fran a great quarterback was his leadership. He exuded

> The thing that made Fran a great quarterback was his leadership.

confidence. He made people around him realize they were winners. Fran has always been a class act, and he was a fine football player who became an outstanding All-Pro and a Hall-of-Famer. Today in professional football you'll see a guy with tremendous ability, but he can't lead. You don't know if the team really has confidence in him. Well, there was no question about that when Fran was with the Vikings and the New York Giants and at Georgia. He was a leader, and everybody knew it. We had great respect and admiration for him.

The thing that impressed me about him as much as anything I've ever seen happened when he was a senior at Athens High School. They played their football games on Friday nights in Sanford Stadium. When I had a chance, I would watch him play. Athens High had won the state championship in their division the year before, but they lost many of their players so Fran's

*In the 1999 **ORANGE BOWL**, Florida beat Syracuse 31-10. Florida coach Steve Spurrier awarded the game ball to himself.

senior year, they weren't that good a football team. One night, they played Baylor Prep of Chattanooga and got the living daylights beat out of them. But Fran threw the ball 55 times in that game, as a senior in high school. I couldn't imagine a high school quarterback throwing the football 55 times. He completed about 35 of them. That was one of the most impressive things I've ever seen a guy do on a night when he got his tail beat. I've told him that many times. Fran's an outstanding guy, a wonderful guy.

Pat Dye was probably the most intense person and player I've ever known. He was the epitome of a football player. He played with us before serving with Bear Bryant for about three or four years at Alabama. When he started out as head football coach at Auburn, there was no question that he would be extremely successful, and he was. Pat Dye was a joy to be around. As a player, he was so fired up. Everything he did was 110 percent, full speed. We played Alabama opening game in '59, and our fullback ran an off-tackle play, broke clean and went about 55 yards for our first touchdown. Pat Dye knocked three people down on that play, and they weren't right at the line of scrimmage. He knocked one down, got up, knocked another one down, then ran downfield and knocked another one down. That's what sold Bear on Pat. After that game, Bear told Pat if he ever wanted to coach he had a job with him, and Pat remembered that. Bear told him that was one of the finest performances he'd ever seen out of a football player, and I have to agree with him. Pat Dye played his heart out. He coached his heart out. Everything he did, he did with his heart.

> Pat Dye was probably the most intense person and player I've ever known.

CLONES ARE PEOPLE TWO

David Pollack

Pollack is a 27-year-old UGA graduate living in Charlotte, North Carolina, with his wife and two children. He graduated from the University in 2005 with a Master of Fine Arts degree in Acting. Here, he recounts what it's like to share a name with one of Georgia's most notable players...a story about what it's like to be "the two and only."

I was in grad school at Georgia the same time the other, more famous, David Pollack played football. I got fan mail sent to my house, but I always tried to send it to him. I also had a lot of people offer to let me stay with them for the Georgia-Florida game down in Jacksonville. I could stay with these fans I had never met—if I was the football player. I never got to meet him, the "real" David Pollack.

While I was at the University, the student paper wrote a review of a play I was in. The article started off focusing on me solely because of my name: something like "No, not that David Pollack." Naturally, I have an affinity for David Pollack. Some people

> That was rather nice because we beat Brett Favre.

have certain numbers that follow them around that they consider lucky. My brother has always picked 47. He was going to have 47 of this or 47 of that; 47 showed up everywhere in his life. My wife and I were watching the 2002 South Carolina game, the game that made David Pollack famous around the country for his interception in the end zone. I looked at the screen and said, "Is that guy named Pollack? Is that a No. 47 on his jersey?" Sure enough, it was David....

The first game I remember going to was the 1990 game against Southern Mississippi in Athens. That was rather nice because we beat Brett Favre. Preston Jones was our quarterback and while he didn't have a stellar NFL career, he managed to beat Favre who had a pretty okay NFL career. It's a nice little notch in the bed post. "I saw Georgia beat Brett Favre! He didn't have the **GREEN BAY PACKERS*** playing with him, but we still beat Brett Favre!"

I really like Eric Zeier, the first true freshman to start at quarterback since World War II. He broke all kinds of records. But the player my family loves to talk about is Zeier's immediate predecessor, Preston Jones. He could throw the ball a thousand miles an hour directly into the ground in front of the receiver's feet or way, way over his head. P. Jones was on the back of his jersey. If somebody threw a Nerf ball wild in our back yard, then we called that a "P. Jones." We still bring him up. He was the quarterback when I started going to games. "Oh, man, P. Jones isn't that great, is he?" we'd say at the games. "No. But we've got this bright kid behind him. Let's wait till next year when they actually bring him in." They brought up Eric Zeier mid-season.

*The Oakland A's colors are green and gold because their late owner, Charles O. Finley, grew up in La Porte, Indiana and loved Notre Dame...when he bought the Kansas City A's, he changed their uniforms to the Notre Dame colors. The GREEN BAY PACKERS also adopted Notre Dame colors because Curly Lambeau played at Notre Dame.

YOU CAN'T GET THIS KIND OF CLARITY WHEN YOU ARE SOBER

Brandon "Bugar" Seely

Seely, 80, lives in Albany, Georgia. He was the Letterman's Association 1997 "Fan of the Year." Bugar is quick to point out that you can't spell Bugar without UGA. He played football on the Georgia All-Star team but was too small to play for the University of Georgia. He played for Stetson University in Florida on what he calls "a little old ding-a-ling scholarship. "

I've had the nickname Bugar since I was six years old. I'd hang around with a bunch of older boys down at the "Y", and I'd jump in their games and mess 'em up. I'd get in trouble, and they'd say, "You're always bugaring everything up." It stuck with me for 70-some-odd years.

In 1975, when we were coming back from the Georgia-Florida game in Jacksonville, we had three couples in a station wagon. We were on Interstate 10, which had just been open for a week or two, and there weren't any filling stations anywhere on it where you could stop and go to the bathroom. We had been drinking beer all day. We went to the game early in the morning and stayed till the partying was done. We won on the last play of the game. A guy ran a flea-flicker and went 75 yards. We were all happy. We were drinking on the way back, but there were no restrooms. We came to an exit and figured there must be a service station. We pulled off the interstate—and no service station. We drove to the bottom of the exit and pulled off the road a little bit. The three men got out and relieved themselves.

About the time we were getting back in the car, here came a police car with its siren on, scaring the hell out of us. We didn't know what in the world he wanted. The policeman was one of those guys—redheaded, bull-necked. We could tell he was really mad because Georgia had upset Florida. He wasn't in any good kind mood for Georgia people. He said, "What do you mean, urinating on my highway?" I said, "What do you mean urinating on your highway? How do you know we were urinating on your highway." He said, "I saw you from right up yonder." I said, "How far is it up there on that hill?" He said, "It's about 300 yards." I said, "300 yards? You saw me?" He said, "Yes, sure, I did." I said, "I'll tell you what I'm going to do. We're going to go to court in Florida before the judge, and I'm going to have the Albany paper there. I'm going to go up to the judge, and I'm going to unzip my britches, and I'm going to lay it out on the table. And, I'm going to say, 'Judge, do you think this man could see this from 300 yards?'" The policeman started getting a little smile, and he said, "I better tear this ticket up, I guess." So, anyway, we didn't get a ticket.

> Just before my head hit on a rock floor downstairs, the cheese-ball rolled under it and kept my head from being busted wide open.

We'd stay at St. Simons Island every year because we didn't want to give our money to Florida. The Georgia folks would always rent houses, and we'd have parties there all week or even two weeks. We'd have a golf tournament called the "Gator Haters Golf Tournament." We didn't care whether you were good, bad or indifferent as far as your golf game was concerned. Ours was more about fun. The big golf tournament they had down there every year would have 700-800 people playing at Jekyll Island. We played at Sea Island on private courses. We had a lot of fun.

My older sister had a condo at St. Simons Island on the beach. She was very, very particular about it. She was a decorator and didn't want anything happening to it. I would have to swear that we would not do anything to mess it up. A group of us stayed there once. After a party one night, which was about four o'clock in the morning, I was climbing my way up the winding stairs to the fourth floor. I had a drink in one hand and a cheese-ball on a plate in the other hand. Just as I got up to the third floor and turned around on the steps, I lost my balance and fell backwards. My arm went through the wall and busted it all the way down. Just before my head hit on a rock floor downstairs, the cheese-ball rolled under it and kept my head from being busted wide open. I didn't spill the drink and I didn't get hurt. My sister wasn't happy at all about the damage. It cost big bucks to fix it and she was never satisfied. She wouldn't let us use it anymore. After several years, she finally gave in, and we were back in her house.

In 1986, we went to Auburn as a big underdog. Georgia upset Auburn 20-16. A large contingent of Georgia fans went down on the playing field to celebrate. The former Georgia groundskeeper who had moved to Auburn turned the automatic sprinklers on us. Then he turned the water hoses on the entire visitors' stands in the end zone where real bulldogs were to try to keep us from coming on the field.

HERSCHEL WALKER WAS JUST A REGULAR GUY WHO SOME DAYS WORE A CAPE

Mike Cavan

Mike Cavan, 60, came to Georgia in '67 and stayed for 19 years as a player and a coach. He was originally from Valdosta and now lives in Athens. He was head football coach at Valdosta State and SMU. His most famous recruit was Herschel Walker.

When Herschel was in high school, he was big and strong—the fastest running back I had ever seen at that time. He was a very humble, polite young man who had been that way all of his life and still is today. He hasn't ever changed. He came from a small town, Wrightsville, and played Class A football. Everybody worried about that, about how good he was going to be because he came from such a small town, but it didn't seem to bother him when he got here, that's for sure.

I watched him some his sophomore year in high school and a lot his junior year and, of course, all of his senior year. That was my area of responsibility. A couple of guys in Wrightsville, Ralph Jackson and Bob Newsome, had been telling me about this kid all along. Most of the time, you find out about a kid because you've been to his school the year before, or somebody from that area will call and tell you.

The main thing we had going for us was UGA was close to his home. He didn't want to get too far away from his mother and father. He came from a great family. His sister was here at the University running track, so that helped. I felt like if we did what we were supposed to do and let him know how badly we needed him and how much we thought of him, we'd get him sooner or later. It worked. He signed Easter Sunday, 1980.

My favorite memories about Herschel Walker are the way he was when he came to Athens, **HOW HARD HE WORKED***, how he never took anything for granted, how tough he was. His first year, we played in the Sugar Bowl for the national championship. On the first play of the game, he dislocated his shoulder. They put it back in, he went right back in the game and carried the ball 35 times. He gained 150 yards against Notre Dame. They hadn't had any back gain over 75 yards all year. He was extraordinary. Nothing bothered him. He played through pain.

Coach Dooley's first year was '64, so his staff was still young when I started playing in 1967. It was a lot of fun playing for him. After I got through playing, I decided I wanted to coach. I went to Coach Dooley, and he put me on as a graduate assistant for a couple of years. I got hired full time in '75. It was good. Then, we built that into a national championship and three straight SEC championships. After that, it was time for me to leave. If I ever wanted to be a head coach, I needed to go. But I had a great time.

> He gained 150 yards against Notre Dame. They hadn't had any back gain over 75 yards all year.

I never knew a guy everybody liked more than Erk Russell. I don't care who you are in the coaching business, somebody doesn't like you, but I never knew a player that came through here who didn't like Coach Russell. He was a tremendous motivator, a great communicator with kids. What he did at Georgia Southern was unbelievable. He went to Georgia Southern when they didn't even have football. They won three national championships with him. One thing I hate for Coach Russell is he never had a chance to

*HERSCHEL WALKER does 3,000 sit-ups daily along with 1500 pushups, while eating only one meal.

coach at a Division 1 school, because I think he'd have had the recognition. I believe he's one of the better coaches ever.

> My livelihood...all my life has been through Georgia football. It's meant everything to me.

Coach Dooley's record speaks for itself. He was outstanding, and a great guy to work for. Coach Dooley's best trait was his consistency. We did everything the same way all the time. We prepared the same way for anybody. It didn't make any difference who we were playing. We could be playing for the national championship. We could be playing a non-conference game. It didn't matter. He was tremendously organized, tremendously prepared, and that's the way he made his team, that's the way he made his coaches. We were prepared. Consequently he didn't lose many games we weren't supposed to. He stayed at Georgia 25 years and won eight games a year—that's what he averaged. That's consistency. That was with far fewer games played each year.

Georgia football means everything to me. It was my way to go to college. It was my college education. I met my wife here. I came here because of football and met her. My children were born here. My livelihood...all my life has been through Georgia football. It's meant everything to me.

OPERATION BULLDOG

Dr. Tommy Lawhorne

Lawhorne, a vascular surgeon, was recruited by coach Ken Cooper and played in Coach Vince Dooley's first class at UGA. He graduated from UGA as valedictorian in 1968, and went on to Johns Hopkins Medical School. Lawhorne is a member of the University Foundation and on the Athletic Board. He is 62 years old and lives in Columbus,

Coach Dooley was a smart, strict disciplinarian. He remains a good friend and someone I respect. He's currently undergoing radiation for a laryngeal carcinoma. The rascal's a workaholic. He's having radiation at seven o'clock every morning, and then he goes to his office! He's got a couple of speaking engagements lined up, even though his voice is a little over a whisper. He's always has been a fierce fighter and competitor.

When Coach Dooley first came to Georgia, he was very severe. He spared his words. Initially, he was sort of a cold fish, to tell you the truth. I was a serious student. I remember getting on the bus once to go to an away game, and he was reading an anthology of American history. I remember wondering how many head coaches on an away trip to a football game would be reading a history anthology like that. He was a very cerebral kind of guy.

ALABAMA* was the reigning national champion. We were playing the reigning national champions on national TV. That was my first game ever, and the first game I ever played in Athens.

---

*In 1966, **ALABAMA** was 12-0. Only 14 of their players weighed over 200 pounds. Their heaviest was 213. In 1980 there was only one NFL player over 300 pounds. In 2008, over 400 NFL players were 300+.

They were a better team. In fact, they went on to win the national championship that year 1965, too. They had a better team, but, that day, we upset them 18-17.

That first game, running on the field in front of over 50,000 fans, I was scared s_ _ _ less. I'd been playing my position, linebacker, for one week. I didn't really know the position very well, and the player I had go against, Paul Crane, was an All-American center. He was a great athlete. It was almost overwhelming to me. I played the game one play at a time. They probably had 40 good athletes. We maybe had about 20 good athletes. We would have lost that game if it had not been on TV. I remember in the fourth quarter, they were driving a couple of times, and we were winded. The network would have a TV timeout that would give us a few minutes to catch our wind, to rest. Without those breaks, a couple of times they probably would have scored.

In some ways, that game was the pinnacle of my career. To go from playing in front of 500 people, at most, on a Friday night in rural Georgia, to playing in front of 50,000-60,000 people in Sanford Stadium, as well as the national television audience—that's a dramatic change in one year. Then to upset the national champions. It was a watershed game. It also was a big step for Dooley. The Dooley era was coming of age. Rather than Georgia being an also-ran, UGA was becoming a competitive/superior program. In '65, we finished 7-3 and did not go to a bowl game.

The next year, in '66, we were 10-1 and our only loss was to Miami on a Friday night at **MIAMI***. Miami always played their home games on Friday night. They beat us 7-6, and we muffed a gimme field goal attempt in the second quarter.

In '67, we probably had a better team than we had in '66, but we didn't play well in a couple of games. We weren't as hungry, and we finished 7-3 and went to the Liberty Bowl, which was an also-ran bowl. We played NC State in Memphis.

*Do you confuse Miami (Ohio) with MIAMI (Florida)? Miami of Ohio was a school before Florida was a state.

Now youngsters are rabid Bulldog fans. But, when I was growing up, Georgia was okay but was not a great football school. The biggest school in the state was Tech. I was a Bobby Dodd disciple. I loved Georgia Tech. I really respected Bobby Dodd. He had good students, *but I saw the light and converted to the Bulldog Nation.*

Georgia Football means a lot of things—friendships, camaraderie. But, it has a bit of a dark side for me. I've had both my knees operated on several times. My hip has been operated on four times. I have four fused vertebras in my neck. My back has been operated on. I'm recovering now from a rotator cuff shoulder surgery. All

> Miami always played their home games on Friday night.

these problems are not related to football per se but I think they have their genesis in football. I was probably too little to play. I played at about 200 pounds. With a proclivity to arthritis, I've paid a hell of a price. I was a vascular surgeon, and in November 2004, I quit operating primarily because I cannot stand at the table long periods of time. I'm working. I'm healthy. I go to work every day, but I can't operate, and that's where the fun of it is.

Overall football has been a wonderful thing for my life, and I love the game. College football has a wonderful mystique. The Georgia Tech game or the Georgia-Auburn game or Georgia-Florida game is always going to be a big game whether they're professional athletes playing it or whether it's just the first 22 kids to get there the day it gets played. In the case of college athletics, particularly college football, its continued success depends on guaranteeing that the participants are genuine students. If they're real students, the game is fun and exciting. But, if the athletes are not legitimate students, the lure of college athletics will subside in hypocrisy. Professional football is fun, but it doesn't have the fanaticism or the camaraderie or the repartee that college football does. Professional athletes are obviously better athletes than at the college level. They play a more intense game, and more is at stake. With college ball it is just a bunch of college kids out playing with one another, it's a different kind of culture....

> ...Uga III, had a salivary gland transplant.

English Bulldogs have what is called a sicca syndrome. They have a lot of dry eyes. The vet school in Athens has done a lot of research with them. In fact, one of the Uga's, I think Uga III, had a salivary gland transplant. They took a salivary gland out of his mouth and put it in his eye to try to help the dryness. They found out that a drug called cyclosporine, the trade name for the eye drops is Restasis, is helpful for patients with sicca syndrome. It's especially useful for people who have had lasik surgery. Many develop sicca syndrome after the surgery, particularly fair-haired women, but it clears up over time. My wife had lasik surgery a couple of years ago, and she really had trouble—had to put drops in her eyes all the time. This Restasis really helped her vision and her comfort. The only downside it has is that she'd put these drops in her eyes, and she'd get in bed at night. I might roll over in bed and hit her sometime during the night, and she would growl and bite me— clamping down on my arm relentlessly.

That just goes to show that truly great comedy is not funny.

RUNNIN' WILD, LOOKIN' PRETTY AND DANCIN' WITH LADY LUCK

Porter Christopher Lady

Lady, 24, lives in Savannah. He went to UGA on a HOPE Scholarship and graduated in 2005. He was a walk-on at Georgia, who later won an Ironman Trophy, the Granite Award and was an Academic All-SEC. He is now well on his way to becoming a master brewer.

I walked on at Georgia in the fall of 2001, just before the season started, almost on a bet. One of my friends said, "Dude, you should walk on. I bet you won't." So, to prove him wrong, I decided to do it. Luckily, they were accepting linemen, so I got a chance to play. I was undersized at only 265 coming in, so one of my difficulties was getting up to size, so I could hold my own during practice. I was going up against 280-300 pound linemen every day in practice. Getting back into the swing of things after not having played football for a year was one of the hardest parts for me. Plus learning the new plays for Georgia and getting acclimated to the intensity of college football compared to high school.

I'd had some interest from Division III schools in Ohio, where one of my coaches had played when he was younger. I didn't want to play for a small school if I was going to play at all, so I declined those offers. Georgia was the primary school I was looking at. The HOPE Scholarship made it extremely affordable for me to go to Georgia and then be able to walk-on. That was a tremendous opportunity for me.

> I was undersized at only 265 coming in, so one of my difficulties was getting up to size...

A group of five of us walked on at the same time. The first day we were in the locker room, we were all sitting there getting ready for practice, just looking at one another, like, "What the hell did we just get ourselves into?" We had a two-day turnaround. We went in, signed the paperwork, got our physicals—then the next day we were told to show up, get our pads, and be back at three o'clock for practice. All of us were stunned. We weren't expecting that kind of turnaround. We had no idea what we had gotten ourselves into, but three of those guys ended up sticking it out with me. That became a group of friends I'll always have.

The first game I suited up for was **HOUSTON*** my freshman year. The Dawg Walk was incredible. We had people on all sides cheering for us as we walked in. Just thinking about how all those people were cheering for me—and no one had ever heard of me and didn't even know what I was doing, but they knew I was playing for Georgia. Then, running out on that field the first time was incredible—90,000 people screaming and hollering as we ran out. There's an adrenalin rush that's hard to explain. You get so hyped up, you think "I hope I don't make a fool of myself running out."

I traveled to one game my senior year, South Carolina. I was amazed at how businesslike it was. I figured there would be more cutting up and laughing and goofing off but, when we got on the bus to head to South Carolina, it was all business. Once we got to the stadium the day of the game, the offensive line was warming up in one of the South Carolina end zones near the student section. We were warming up and going through our pre-game motions. The fans behind us were screaming and shouting. Then, all of a sudden, empty cups were being thrown at us. I thought, "You've got to be kidding me." We couldn't believe they were so rude that they would throw cups and trash at us. At Georgia the opposing team would get booed, but they wouldn't get anything thrown at them.

*The **HOUSTON** Astros, then called the Colt 45s, debuted in 1962. Their public address announcer that season was Dan Rather....The public address announcer for the Brooklyn Dodgers in 1937-'38 was John Forsythe, the actor.

My best memories are after practice when all the offensive linemen would go sit on the benches outside the locker room. We'd sit there for 15-20 minutes resting after a long practice, joking around and hanging out.

The Iron Man Award was for not missing a single practice from the beginning of spring drills in January until the last bowl practice. As a walk-on, I worked all year without a lot of the recognition. Before I even knew it, it was three-fourths of the way through the season. One of the trainers came up to me and said, "Hey, man you only have four more games to go and you've got an Iron Man Trophy." I said, "What?" I looked on this giant board in the locker room that, at the beginning of the year, had all the players' names on it. Three-quarters of the way through the season, there were only 15-20 guys' names left on the board. Just knowing I had made it that far was really encouraging. I won the award along with eight other players. Getting my picture taken with all the guys and Coach Richt at the Senior Gala was pretty cool.

...he'd yell, "Get your little Savannah butt ..."

During the spring and summer right before my senior year and throughout my senior season, Coach Richt would have all the seniors over to his house to hang out with his family. They'd grill out for us. We played Pac-Man and pool down in his basement. He had the old-school coin-fed arcade games down there.

Coach Callaway was my position coach. For the first year, he didn't know my name but he knew where I was from. Anytime I messed up, he'd yell, "Get your little Savannah butt ..." I could see him try to think of my name, but nothing came out except for where I was from. The next spring when I was involved more with position meetings he got to know me.

The first time I played, Coach Callaway turned to me and said, "Get ready to go in. You're going in on the next series." Running out on the field during the next possession and hearing the crowd again gave me an adrenalin kick. I felt like I could do anything. Getting into stance and getting ready to go, it really gets you going. Once you're out on the field, it gets quiet because you're so focused. The crowd has gotten you so focused that you almost block the noise out. At least, that's how it was for me.

I never got to travel with the team for the Georgia-Florida game, but I was there every year. My senior year was the first time we won in a long time. It capped off that season. Since I didn't play in those games, I had the opportunity to partake in the festivities. I went down to The Landing a couple of nights before the game to see all the people jam-packed into it. One side is Georgia. The other side is Florida. If one person starts a Georgia cheer, every one does it. Once we'd get done, the Florida people would cheer. It went back and forth for hours.

After one of those Landing experiences, half of our group got a cab home, while the rest of us stayed downtown. We ended up stuck there until five o'clock in the morning, trying to find a cab. We kept running into other fans doing the same thing. We were all thinking how we should be resting for the game the next day. It was verging on one of those Seinfeld-ridiculous moments. How could we not get a ride home?

The past couple of years I've been going down with a group of 15-20 friends. The family we stayed with the last time we went has a divided house. The mom went to Florida. The dad went to Georgia. Their daughter went to Georgia. That's how we've gotten to go down there. We were tailgating in the Florida parking lot at the stadium. Of course, we had all our Georgia flags flying and Georgia tents and everyone was wearing red and black in the midst of this sea of blue and orange. A little girl about four years old was on the other side of the lane we were parked on, and she was looking at us. She had this scowl on her face like we were the enemy. We did a Georgia chant. She did the Gator chomp. We laughed. She was so serious, saying "Go Florida. Go Gators," and doing the chomp. We walked over to her and said that wasn't nice for her to be doing that. "Can we get you to do one 'Go Dawg?'" She said, "No," and almost cried. She ran back to her parents. We were amazed that the rivalry starts at such a young age. Just the thought of doing one Georgia chant for us almost made her cry. That is Georgia-Florida. That's how ingrained it is.

The first year I was out of school, it was sad to go to the game and be in the stands. I was so used to being out on the field. I was thinking, "Wow! I really do miss it." Right after my last season ended, I thought, "I'm done! I don't have to practice. I have all this time. I'm free." Then when the season rolled around again, I realized how much it meant to me and how much I missed it. There was that little sadness knowing I wasn't going to be playing any more. But, now, after being away from it for a couple of years, it's nice to go back and appreciate what those guys on the field are doing and all the work they put in. I just go in and cheer as hard as I can.

> The first year I was out of school, it was sad to go to the game and be in the stands.

I remember Dad's friend, Don Sullivan, when I lived in Marietta. He said, "One thing you've got to get really good at is being a long snapper. Everyone needs a long snapper. There are never that many good long snappers out there. Who knows? It could take you pro." I remember him being so excited about me being first a center, and then knowing I could long snap. He said, "That's your ticket. Run with it." One spring Georgia was searching for a long snapper. I went out and snapped a couple of times, but I hadn't done it for a couple of years. I was rusty, so I didn't make it. I did it all through high school, but I didn't make long snapper at Georgia, which was perfectly fine with me. I was happy doing the normal center. I should have listened to Mr. Sullivan. He's a genius.

Georgia football, for me, was something I will never forget. The people I got to meet, the coaches, the other players, friendships that will last forever. Knowing all the blood, sweat and tears you've spent with those others guys is just amazing. The brotherhood that is Georgia football is one of those things that will stick with me forever. I look forward to being able to watch many, many games now from the stands and know what those guys went through to get ready. Whenever I hear about Georgia football, I've got to speak up because I was Georgia football for four years.

In the South, if you ask people what football team they cheer for, they automatically say whatever college they support. You ask someone in Georgia or South Carolina, you're not going to hear the Atlanta Falcons or the Carolina Panthers, you're going to hear South Carolina or Georgia. You go up north, like Chicago, or out West or wherever, and ask what football team they cheer for, you hear Giants, Bears or **49ers.*** I always think how amazing it is that for people in the South, football always means college football.

> The brotherhood that is Georgia football is one of those things that will stick with me forever.

*When the 49ers checked into their hotel before the 1982 Super Bowl, their head coach, the late Bill Walsh, greeted them disguised as a bellhop.

BILLY PAYNE'S FUTURE IS HISTORY

William Porter (Billy) Payne

Payne, 60, UGA '69 UGA Law '73 is the man credited with bringing the 1996 Olympics to Atlanta. Billy's father Porter was a player at Georgia in the late '40s and was a close friend of Coach Wally Butts.

My dad and mom went to the University of Georgia and immediately had two children. One of the difficulties was trying to be a dad and a husband and play ball and go to school at the same time. My dad developed an incredible relationship with Coach Butts, to the point where Coach Butts or his family would help out. Or he would get other people to help babysit us kids so my mom could go to the games, even when they were out of town. They developed a pretty close relationship. My dad, to his last moment, always possessed incredible positive memories of Coach Butts and their relationship.

My dad didn't have any money, and he had to support two kids and a wife. Back then, the athletes would eat in a certain cafeteria during the day. They were entitled, as a scholarship player, to have their meals provided. Coach Butts, the last couple of years, gave my dad a key to the cafeteria so he could go back in the kitchen in off hours and get enough food to feed his family.

> Coach Butts... gave my dad a key to the cafeteria so he could go back in the kitchen in off hours and get enough food to feed his family.

Later my dad was a Southeastern Conference football official. As a consequence, he would be invited by Coach Butts every year to officiate at the spring game and some of the summer practices. He would always take me with him, so I had a long history of being on the field with the players.

I was a mascot, and I remember all the players at that time were aware of my dad, and the success he'd had years earlier at Georgia. I was just a little kid, six to ten years old. I remember sitting in their laps and on their knees a lot during some of the scrimmages.

In my early teenage years, because of my long connection with Georgia, I aspired to play football there. As I got closer and closer to my junior and senior years, and it became apparent I'd have an opportunity to go wherever I wanted to go, I entertained the thought of not going to Georgia because everybody would assume it was because I wanted to follow in my father's footsteps. I seriously considered the **UNIVERSITY OF TEXAS***, Notre Dame, University of Florida and Auburn. However, as I progressed through my senior year, it became apparent that I couldn't walk away from the love and affection I had developed throughout my life for the University of Georgia. It was a part of me, and that's where I had to go.

When I went to Georgia, it was one of the last years freshmen could not play on the varsity. I went in the fall of '65 and played on the freshman team. Then, I was on the varsity '66, '67, and '68 seasons.

Coach "Doc" Ayers was a great motivator. We had a terrific freshman team. We murdered everybody we played, and it was one of the great recruiting classes that we ever had. Coach Ayers says it may be the second best he ever had. His coaching philosophy was that he was going to find the best 22 players, irrespective of what positions they had played in high school and put them on the field.

I had been a quarterback in high school and had some success. In the summer between graduating from high school and going

*When Mack Brown was named head coach at the UNIVERSITY OF TEXAS, he became the highest paid college coach ever, even though he had never even won a conference championship.

to college, there was a high school All-Star football game where north Georgia high school players played south Georgia players. When I showed up for that, there were three quarterbacks on the north team. The coach, Bill Chapel from Dalton High School, came up to the three of us quarterbacks and said, "Y'all are all pretty good, but only one of you is going to get to play. Any of y'all want to play another position so you can be in there for the whole game?" I raised my hand and said, "I don't care where I play, I just want to play every play." He said, "Well, you're going to be an end," which I had never played before. I played end that game and had some success. Of course, the Georgia coaches were all in attendance, so by the time I got to Georgia, I was an end. I never played quarterback again.

> I raised my hand and said, "I don't care where I play, I just want to play every play."

Frank Inman was my position coach during the first two years on the varsity, where I played offensive end. My last year, when I switched to defense, my position coach was Jim Pyburn. The defensive coordinator was Erk Russell.

Coach Inman was a tireless worker. He was a perfectionist. He would require us to run the plays over ad nauseam until we got them right. The thing that bothered him the most was players who took it easy when the play was called to the other side and didn't go downfield and block and do all those things. He would make us run 50 yards. There could be an off-tackle slant to the other side—we'd have to go 50 yards downfield looking for somebody to block. He was obsessed with downfield blocking.

In 1968 we played the University of Florida in the **GATOR BOWL*** in Jacksonville. They had a great team that year. We had an exceptionally good team that year as well. It must have rained

*The Six "R's" of BOWL Selection: Records, Rankings, Ratings, Rewards, Reverence and Rematch.

four or five inches during the game. We ended up winning 52-0. What had been a pretty even game going in turned to a rout in the rain. We got so far ahead during the first half, that me and Bill Stanfill, our great All-American Outland trophy winner defensive tackle, were taken out of the game. At the time, I was playing defense, and he and I were on the end of that line. For the previous two series, we were winning by so much that Coach Dooley had put the second string in already. Bill and I figured we weren't going to play anymore that half...we were so wet that we left the field to go to the locker room to change jerseys. Lo and behold, we'd been inside about two minutes and were bragging about how smart we were to get out of that horrible rain, when in came Coach Russell. He went ballistic. It was unbelievable. He was so mad at us he could have killed us. His punishment was he made us cover the kickoff for the second half. The good players are not supposed to cover the kickoffs because you can get hurt. I think we both took about two steps and stopped.

> We were bragging about how smart we were to get out of that horrible rain, when here came Coach Russell. He went ballistic. It was unbelievable.

Coach Russell was the best motivator of young men I've ever encountered. His way was to motivate by example. When he would show us where we were supposed to stick our heads in a tackle, he would go do it without his helmet and come away, as you've heard a million times, a bloody mess. You would follow him anywhere. You'd follow him into a raging fire. Coach Russell went south a few years after I played to coach so successfully at Georgia Southern. I went to several of the games to tell him how proud I was of him. I attended his funeral a couple of years ago with hundreds of other Georgia players. It was a great tribute to a great man.

On road trips, we had our game faces on, and it was disciplined. We didn't have any time to get in trouble. We showed up with one thing in mind, and that was to win the game. Fortunately, we won

98 percent of them while I was playing. So usually the plane ride back was a happy one, but not humorous—we left it all out on the field. When it was over with, there was not a whole lot of laughing going on.

The stadium we played at on a regular basis that I thought showed the greatest loyalty to the home team was Auburn. They were passionate about their teams. Very similar to the way Sanford Stadium would be when we were the home team. I thought it was a great place to play.

Sonny Seiler and I have been friends forever. I've been through a lot of Ugas in my career. I'm the Chairman of Augusta National Golf Club. I have had the pleasure several times since I've been a member to invite some of the coaches over to play with me. That's always been fun.

I've been close with all the Georgia coaches, but nothing like with Coach Dooley. Coach Richt is a man of great faith. He's a man with a very highly developed and much appreciated value system. I would stand in line to get one of my children to play for him. He brings to the University of Georgia the class, the sophistication and the character that we would all aspire to have in a coach leading such an important program.

Coach Donnan and Coach Goff were both coaching when I was doing the Olympics and working so hard. There was a period there where I was so busy I couldn't go to many games. They are all personal friends of mine and I respect the contributions they've made to Georgia. They are good men.

I'm the kind of fan who doesn't get too involved in the game because I don't want to start critiquing or doing any of that. I don't try to be an armchair quarterback. I just go for the experience. I love to see the crowds. I love to see the red and black. I love to win. Mostly, I go to enjoy the game.

I don't go to many road games, but I always go to the Florida game in Jacksonville, always. When we were trying to get the Olympics, we had various delegates from around the world visit

Atlanta to show them what we could offer. One of the times, the IOC, International Olympic Committee, member from Bulgaria was visiting Atlanta the same weekend as the Georgia-Florida game. I told him I was going to take him to the game, "I want you to see American football." He had never seen it. He was blown away by the atmosphere and the crowds. We had him barking like a dog before it was over. It was quite an experience. There's nothing in football like the Georgia-Florida game. It's an incredibly intense loyalty, a great environment and a fun time for all.

> I would put friendships at the very top of the list of what Georgia means to me.

Georgia football, more than anything, allowed me the opportunity to make some wonderful friends who have remained important parts of my life for the last 40 years. I would put friendships at the very top of the list of what Georgia means to me. Secondarily, I would say it taught me some discipline and a work ethic that have benefited me throughout my life. Thirdly, I would say that the mere fact I went to the University of Georgia was more important than the fact that I played football at Georgia because it's such a great institution. I'm proud to have been a part of the team.

THERE IS NO EXPIRATION DATE ON DREAMS

John Barnett

Barnett, 50, graduated from Augusta State University in 1979. He is a football coach and history teacher at Thomson High School in Thomson, Georgia.

I am the defensive coordinator at Thomson High School and coached Danny Verdun his entire high school career, 1999-2002. We had a lot of good times together and a lot of success, winning 42 games during his four-year, high school career. His senior year we won the state championship.

Danny was always very goal-oriented. He knew he wanted to be a good enough football player to play in the SEC. It used to worry me that his brother sent him to a lot of camps at Florida, Tennessee, Auburn and Georgia. I was afraid he would get hurt. Dang if he didn't. He was in a camp at Tennessee and he re-injured a foot that he had a hairline fracture on. This was before his junior season. He had to have surgery to put a pin in his foot. He and I have talked about this—he didn't play as well his junior year as everybody expected him to. He started practicing about a week before the first game and really wasn't in good shape. But he kept his eye on the prize, to be an SEC football player.

Even when he was in the ninth grade, I could tell Danny had a little something special. He was very in tune to the game. I told him I should have started him as a freshman, but I didn't want to throw him to the wolves. He really developed over a

> It used to worry me that his brother sent him to a lot of camps at Florida, Tennessee, Auburn and Georgia.

period of time and became more serious about his schoolwork. He always made good grades.

> I would get so aggravated when things weren't going well, my wife wouldn't want to talk to me...

We were in the middle of his senior year, and he knocked on my classroom door. We had a big game coming up that week, our chief rival for the region championship. I said, "Danny, is something wrong?" He said, "No, coach, I just wanted to tell you that I just committed to Georgia. I wanted to go ahead and get it over with, so I could concentrate on beating Statesboro." And we did. That is a special memory that he thought enough of me to come and tell me right after he'd made his decision. He told me that Coach Richt would be here on a certain date. Then, he made a point of introducing me to Coach Richt. He's a special kid. The rest is history. He went on to have a great career at Georgia.

I quit going to games in Athens because I couldn't behave. I would get so aggravated when things weren't going well that my wife wouldn't want to talk to me all the way home. I figured I could make a fool of myself in the privacy of my own home and not embarrass my wife and my daddy and other people who were with us.

My wife is a Tennessee graduate. Back in the '90s I think Tennessee beat Georgia nine straight times. I referred to the Georgia-Tennessee week as my annual humiliation. She's a very good sport about all this and has never kidded me about it.

I started going back to games when Danny started playing in 2003. He was a freshman, and somebody called me at the last minute and told me they had an extra ticket for the Georgia-Alabama game. I got in touch with Danny's mom and said, "If you talk to him, tell him I'm going to be at the game." I had heard an inkling that he might get a chance to start—he was a true freshman. He never redshirted.

I remember the feeling I had that day when Danny was announced as a starter, and his face came up on that big screen there in the stadium. That was one of the proudest moments I've ever had as a football coach. They ended up winning the game that day against Alabama. It was a great, great experience for me.

With my schedule, I didn't get to go up but once or twice a year while he was playing. When I got to go up for a game, I would go to the Dawg Walk. Danny would always come over and hug me before he went in. That always made me feel about ten feet tall.

College football in the South is different than other places. If you're a college football fan, your whole outlook, your whole attitude can depend on how your team did. In my case, I have a double whammy. My first priority, of course, has to be my high school team winning on Friday night. It's a great feeling to wake up Sunday morning and know that my Thomson Bulldogs won on Friday night and the Georgia Bulldogs won on Saturday. That's euphoria for me.

> College football in the South is different than other places.

ROOTIN' FOR GEORGIA
IS LIKE PLAYIN' HOOKY FROM LIFE

Candler Meadors

Meadors has come a long way since he was a young Georgia Tech fan selling Coca-Colas at Grant Field. Eventually, he saw the light and graduated from UGA in 1951. For 25 years he has been the Executive Secretary of the Athens Touchdown Club. He has been in the car business for 38 years, the last 12 as a Mercedes and Volkswagen dealer in Athens.

The first time I saw Georgia play was in 1946. We played Oklahoma State, which, at that time, was Oklahoma A&M. Oklahoma A&M had an All-American, Bob Fenimore, at tailback. Then we played Alabama with Harry Gilman, who was an All-American. Then, of course, we played Tech, and the star player for Tech was Frank Broyles, the recently retired athletic director at Arkansas.

I played high school football and went to Athens for my first game with my high school coach. The stadium was not anything like it is today. It could seat probably 40,000 then it was a big experience. I had played a couple of high school games in Jacksonville. We played Robert E. Lee in the Gator Bowl. It was a high school game, but at the Gator Bowl, which at that time didn't seat but about 25,000. Then we played Miami in the Orange Bowl in a Milk Bowl game, and the Orange Bowl was bigger than the Gator Bowl.

I have not missed but one Georgia-Auburn game since 1958. I had to go to a wedding back in the early sixties, which caused me to miss one. I've seen some great ball games in Auburn and also here. I've been to all the stadiums in the SEC except Mississippi

State. **LSU*** on Saturday night is a great, great, great thrill. I was down there in '78 when we beat LSU in a big upset. Lindsay Scott ran the second-half kickoff back for a touchdown. The Conference, wherever you go, is going to be a great experience.

Sanford Stadium with the hedges is a beautiful stadium. It's not like a lot of stadiums that started off beautiful when they were built but have been added to and added to over the years. The beauty of the stadium in Athens is the hedges, and the history of that place is awesome.

Francis Tarkenton is a long-time friend of mine. I watched Fran when he played high school football here at Athens and then at Georgia. His daddy and mother were great friends of mine. We were in the same church with Mrs. Tarkenton before she died.

> They were having a hard time selling season tickets, so about 150 guys here started the Touchdown Club...

The Athens Touchdown Club recently celebrated its 60th anniversary. We started in 1946. It was an organization started by the athletic department to sell tickets. They were having a hard time selling season tickets, so about 150 guys here started the Touchdown Club, and we've kept it in existence all this time. I'm just the third secretary we've had. The job keeps me close to the football program. We exist to help in any way we legally can with the football program in Georgia. I've gotten to know a ton of players. Guys like Andy Johnson, who played here at Athens High School and Francis and some of those guys are a little bit closer because I saw them play high school ball.

I was very fortunate to see Charley Trippi's last football game in the Stadium against Georgia Tech. We beat them 35-7. That was

*What Heisman Trophy winner has made the most money? The 1959 winner, Billy Cannon of <u>LSU</u>, was arrested for counterfeiting in the early '80s and spent almost three years in jail. Technically, he is the only Heisman Trophy winner to ever "make" money.

the Georgia team that went on to play **NORTH CAROLINA*** with Charlie "Choo Choo" Justice in the Sugar Bowl. We won that game 20-10. Charlie played 60 minutes that day—60 minutes! He did not come out of the ball game. He did everything. A lot of people don't realize this, but Charlie has been voted on some of these all-time All-SEC teams as a defensive back. He was a great, great defensive player, and not only that, he was a tailback. They ran single wing and a little bit of T. He kicked. He threw the ball. He ran the ball. And he played great defense. His was one of the greatest performances I had ever seen by a Georgia player.

> Herschel was one of a kind, and, by the way, a humble, tremendous individual.

Of course, I have a lot of memories about Francis Tarkenton. I was at the Georgia-Auburn game in 1959 when he threw the pass in the last minute to Bill Herron for a touchdown, and Delbert Pennington kicked the extra point, and we won the SEC championship. That is one of my big memories of Francis.

Herschel—aw man, you can just call them out. I saw so many of his great runs and his great games. Herschel was one of a kind, and, by the way, a humble, tremendous individual. Every time I see him, he walks up to me, and he hugs me. He's very down to earth. We had him at the Touchdown Club about five years ago. We have our meetings at the Country Club, and we had a record crowd that night. It was incredible the people who brought stuff for him to sign. For about 30 minutes after the meeting he signed everything anybody had to sign, whether it was a helmet, a piece of paper, a program, a jersey or whatever. He was as cordial and as nice signing the last one as he was signing the first one. He's an unusual guy.

---

*Michael Jordan was given his first set of golf clubs by fellow University of **NORTH CAROLINA** classmate, Davis Love, Davis Love, Davis Love.... The Roman Guy.

Francis has been back, too. He was a master of ceremonies when we celebrated our 50th anniversary. We had a black-tie banquet down at the Classic Center. He doesn't get over here as much as he used to. He has done a lot to raise money for different charity organizations. He's been very, very successful in business. He's a great salesman. He can stand up and talk in front of people. His daddy was a Baptist minister, so he was trained right. He was not a great, great athlete. I remember that. Although, in high school he played basketball, football and baseball. Certainly, he was not a great athlete when he played professional football, but he still has some passing records that haven't been broken....

My favorite trip was back in 1959, to the Georgia-Florida game. Francis was quarterback, and Charlie Britt also played quarterback. We played in a drizzling rain. It was a cold day in the Gator Bowl. Charlie Britt intercepted a pass about three yards in the end zone and ran it 103 yards for a touchdown. It was a great, great football game. It was a great trip because of winning the ball game, and because on the way back we stayed at St. Simons at the King and Prince Hotel. Walking into that big hotel with the big fire in the lobby on that cold night was great....

...but I said, "Vince, who?"... Nobody had ever heard of Vince Dooley....

Vince Dooley and I have been friends a long time. I worked with him closely through the Touchdown Club. Used to be, when you went out to eat with him, you'd always have to buy the meal. He called me a couple of times to tell me he wanted to have lunch with me, and I wound up paying for the meal. That's the way Vince is. He's close with the dollar. I enjoyed going to practice and enjoyed watching him operate on the practice field. He's always been very cordial and a first-class gentleman.

We played Georgia Tech in Atlanta at the end of the 1964 season. I went from Grant Field to the airport and flew to Detroit for a two-week management school with Chevrolet Motor Division. We had about 40 retail people from all over the country there.

Tuesday morning I was in the hotel restaurant eating breakfast and the general manager of a big Chevrolet store in El Paso, Texas, sat down with me. He said, "Well, I see you got a new football coach at Georgia." I said, "We have?" He said, "Yeah. Vince Dooley." Now, you're not going to believe this, but I said, "Vince, who?" Of course, everybody said that at first. Vince had been an assistant coach at Auburn. Nobody had ever heard of Vince Dooley....

> It was the only basketball arena in the world where the wind was a factor...

I am a real Bulldog—football, basketball, baseball—I have season tickets to all of them. I've done the stats for the basketball games for 20 years. That's part of my life. I've seen so many great, great basketball players come through. I saw Pistol Pete play for three years. Dominique Wilkins—I got to meet when he was here, and we've become good friends. A number of great, great players came into the Coliseum. Our basketball program has not been quite on the level with our football program. Still, it's been pretty good. I've still got my four original tickets in the Coliseum.

We built the Coliseum and opened it, I believe, in '63. It has the big beams that go across and are in the ground. We only lived about six blocks from the arena, so we watched them when they shoveled the first dirt. The first thing they did, they put four crossbows that go all the way across. The ceiling is triangles. They put it together like a jigsaw puzzle. You go inside and look up, and you can see how the pieces fit together, and they were all numbered. I've got some pictures of the kids walking up the crossbows as far as they could.

Georgia had been playing in Woodruff Hall, a wooded building that held about 2,500 people. It was the only basketball arena in the world where the wind was a factor in shooting the basketball because the building had so many cracks in it. I've been over there when it started raining and we had to put buckets out to catch the water. Red Lawson was the coach. Red and I became good friends when I first came to Athens, and I never bought a ticket to Woodruff Hall. Red always gave me two tickets. Most of the time, it wasn't a sellout, so I never bought a ticket.

We opened with Tech, in the middle of the season at the Coliseum, around February of '62. It was the largest crowd we've ever had in the Coliseum, because we had people sitting in the aisles. The fire marshal really raised hell about it afterwards. That opening game was a sellout. About four o'clock in the afternoon, I realized I didn't have any tickets. They had already announced it was a sellout. I was working, and we were playing Tech that night and opening the Coliseum. I called Red, and he left me two tickets at the box office. From then on, I've had the same four tickets for every game.

I've never seen a player who loved to play the game and loved to practice like Dominique Wilkins. Recently Dominique was inducted into the Hall of Fame. The *Atlanta Journal Constitution* had a great section on him, a big full-page spread, including a full-page photo. He had on a suit and tie...*and he had on tennis shoes.* He was driving in for a lay-up. They talked to Coach Hugh Durham, and they had a paragraph or two they wrote about Dominique. Every single one of them said the exact thing I'm saying. Mr. O'Toole, the trainer, said he never had any problems with Dominique wanting to go out and practice, even if he was hurt. He had a hard time keeping him in. All the coaches he played for made that same statement that they had never seen anybody they had coached that loved—*loved* to play the game like he did. If he'd had to, he would probably have played it for nothing. He's a great guy. I was at one of the Hawks games when he was still playing, so it was a long time ago. One of my friends had season tickets close in behind the home bench. Dominique had a separated shoulder or something, I can't remember exactly. He was not even in uniform. He was dressed in street

> I've never seen a player who loved to play the game and loved to practice like Dominique Wilkins.

clothes and sitting on the bench. We were sitting about 15 rows back, and he saw me. He came up to where I was and shook hands with me and hugged me. I'm real happy for what he's done and how he's been a success. He's an officer with the Hawks now.

I knew both Terrell Davis and Champ Bailey real well when they played here. Terrell didn't have a real good career at Georgia. He was playing at a school in California that gave up football. I can't remember how Terrell got here. But he came here and we thought he was going to be a great halfback. Then he pulled a hamstring. He didn't stay here but two years. He never got really, really healthy with that hamstring. Coach Goff was the coach. Hamstrings affect guys differently. I could have a bad hamstring and get over it pretty quick, because maybe that's just my makeup. You could have a bad hamstring, and it could bother you for two or three months. The first year Terrell was here, he didn't do much. But, he showed promise.

I used to take my kids to picture day before the season would start. My granddaughter, now 26 years old, has a picture of Terrell Davis giving her his helmet. She put his helmet on, and we took a picture. He was drafted in the sixth round and became a great, great player. We've got people around here that say, "Well, Coach Goff didn't know what he was doing." Well, that's a bunch of crap. You know good and well Ray wouldn't play him hurt. It just didn't work out. It did work out for him in the pros, and I'm so happy that it did.

Champ Bailey is from Folkston, Georgia, down on the Georgia-Florida border, on Highway 15, going into Jacksonville. People go through there to see the alligators and the snakes. We heard about Champ when he was in high school. He was one of those great, great players. He may be the best defensive guy we've had since I've been watching Georgia. He has a brother, Boss, a linebacker with Detroit. Boss was really a better athlete than Champ. That's hard to believe, but that's what the coaches told me when they were recruiting both of them. Boss got hurt on the first or second kick-off in the opening ball game. I don't know why they were playing him on the kick-off team because you can get hurt like that. He got a knee injury that knocked him out for that year. Before that season I was in the training room. I had hurt my knee. I went to see the trainer and happened to be in the training room when a big cheer broke out. Somebody ran in and told me that Boss had just broken the all-time vertical leap record for the football team. He was a great athlete. I think he still holds the vertical-jump record.

> No stadium in college football compares with Tennessee's Neyland...

That's taking nothing away from Champ because Champ's a great player, too. Champ signed that last contract, when he went to Denver, for about $60 million. I don't know what Boss signed for. I'm sure he got $25 million. So, both of them could probably buy their little town. They also had another brother, who was a good player, too, but he didn't pan out at Georgia.

No stadium in college football compares with Tennessee's Neyland Stadium simply because, you've got 107,000 folks crammed in. A lot of my friends don't like to go to Knoxville because they claim the seats are so small you can hardly sit down. I've always had great experiences up there. It's always a great football game.

Georgia athletics has meant a lot to me. When you get my age, all you have left is memories. I thoroughly enjoyed the automobile business. I go to car shows. I've got automobiles in my blood. But, the athletic program, next to my family and next to my church, has been a real part of my life since I came to Athens. Georgia is a football school. That's why we have a 92,000-seat football stadium. It's been a great part of my life and I've enjoyed every single minute of it. I'll hate the day, if I live long enough, that I won't be able go to football games, and I'll have to watch them on TV.

FANECDOTES

When I was going through rush, I met Bill Stanfill, a member of my fraternity. He was the biggest, most impressive man I'd ever seen in my whole life. He was probably 6'4", 240 pounds, back in 1966. He was the biggest player in the SEC at the time. His hands were as big as catchers' mitts. To an 18-year-old kid, fresh from home, he seemed like **ANDRE THE GIANT***! He was a big old teddy bear type guy. He was really a kind of gentle giant, personally, but he was a beast on the field.

—*GREG GRIFFIN*, Attorney Marietta, GA

One time, a lady whose daughter was a cheerleader was sitting in the stands. An African-American couple was sitting next to her. She said to the couple when they introduced the cheerleaders before the game, "That's my daughter." The lady said, "Oh, I know you're proud of her." She said, "Uh-huh, look at her." The proud mother told all about her daughter, how she was a good student, and what sorority she had pledged. She was talking on and on as the game got started. About two or three plays into the game, Herschel Walker got the ball and took off for a 76-yard run. Everybody all around was jumping and screaming and everything. The second lady leaned over to the first and said, "That's my son." The cheerleader's mother said she could have crawled under the stadium because she had been promoting her daughter so much.

—CLAUDE MCBRIDE, Chaplain, Fellowship of Christian Athletes

In 1967, George Patton was first team All-American for Georgia. My father signed Patton from a small high school in Alabama to play for Georgia. My father recruited in the days when alumni could recruit. Mr. and Mrs. Patton were not in great health, so they asked my mother and father if I could drive them from

---

*Wrestler **ANDRE THE GIANT** was 7'4" tall and weighed 520 pounds. He passed away in North Carolina in January of 1993.

ALABAMA* out to Dallas, Texas, for the Cotton Bowl. I was 17 years old at the time. I had a little allergy to smoke, and Mr. Patton smoked a lot of cigarettes. I drove the Pattons, and my father, mother, and another couple were in another car. Every time we stopped, I said to my dad, "You need to drive them. The smoke's driving me crazy."

George was a 6'3," 215-pound quarterback in high school in the mid-sixties and nobody offered him a scholarship. Georgia took a chance on him, and he turned out to be a first-team All-American defensive end. He never played quarterback at Georgia. When he was a senior at Georgia, the day before the Cotton Bowl, Mr. Patton told us that Coach Dooley told George that if Georgia got ahead, they were going to let him play quarterback at the end of the game. He had made All-American two years in a row, and he wanted to throw a pass in college. Georgia got ahead real fast and held on.

At the game, we were sitting next to people we didn't know. I was a cocky 17-year-old. I started telling the people next to me, "I bet you George Patton is going to play quarterback today." They said, "George Patton is a defensive end." I said, "No. He was a quarterback in high school. I think they're going to put him in at quarterback." When he came on the field as a quarterback at the end of the game, these people looked at me. You could tell they were thinking, "How in the world did he know that?" They started telling the people next to them. All of them were looking at me, wanting to know how in the world I knew. He had never played one play at quarterback. How did I know he was going to play at quarterback in the bowl game? People kept asking me how I knew. Finally, I told them.

—**TOM CLOUD**, 57, Alpharetta, GA

Tommy Lawhorne, Georgia linebacker in the late '60s, made one "A" while at Georgia. The rest of his grades were A-pluses. He was so smart. Once he locked in on studying you could set a bomb off behind him and he wouldn't even hear it.

This is a 19-year-old kid we're talking about. We got to playing with each other—that "last tag, no tag back" game. He would be

*Mike Dubose is the only native **ALABAMAN** to coach the Crimson Tide.

> He reached over and slapped me on the hand and said, "Last tag, no tag back."

at the library studying and I'd be in my room already asleep. When the library would close, he'd come in my room, we never locked our doors. He'd slap me awake and say, "Last tag, no tag back." We were always trying to get each other with that.

When he finished up his residency, he came through Statesboro, where I lived. When we got together, I was sitting there the whole time, thinking, "I need to get him last tag." I thought, "No, he's a doctor now. We've outgrown that." We spent about an hour together. He started to leave, and we had not seen each other for probably eight years. He said, "Bruce." I said, "What?" He reached over and slapped me on the hand and said, "Last tag, no tag back." I said, "You don't know how bad I wanted to do that, but I thought we were too mature."

Later when my wife had Hodgkin's disease, he was the first person I called. Once they started the process of determining what stage it was in, he wanted to know everything that was going on and he called and checked on us. So, there's a serious side to both of us, too.

—BRUCE YAWN, Offensive lineman at UGA '66-'68

When I went to the NFL, there weren't that many other Bulldogs playing in the pros. My teammate, Jake Scott, joined us my second year in Miami. He and I were always real close. Jake had a ranch in Colorado, north of Glenwood Springs. I went up there hunting with him two or three years after I retired. We had gotten back to his pickup truck and we both put our guns on the seat between us. When I got in, my butt hit one of the guns. It went off and shot a hole through the floorboard. Jake was fuming. He was mad as hell about me putting my loaded gun in the truck. I said, "Hell, I unloaded mine. You better check yours, buddy." We checked our guns, and, sure enough, it was his that had discharged. By this time, you could hear the air coming out of the right front tire where the bullet had gone through it. He got out, and I needled him a little, like he had been getting on me. "Jake, just think of all the money you saved," I said. "What the hell are you talking about?" he said. "Look at all the money you saved in taxidermy," I said. "What?" he asked. "That tire's already mounted on that rim," I said.

—BILL STANFILL, All-American and Outland Trophy winner, '66-'68

I have a sentimental connection to the Chicago Bears, which takes me back to the likes of Terry Hoage, Bill Leary, Jeff Sanchez and Kevin Butler. Kevin came home from his rookie season with the Bears credited with 11 kicker tackles and wearing a Super Bowl ring. One afternoon, not long thereafter, my phone rang and the receptionist said, "There's a fellow calling who identifies himself as 'the Butler,' and says he wants to speak to you." I immediately recognized the voice of Davis Butler, Kevin's father, "Bennigan's, five o'clock—be there or be square." Needless to say I was there at five, where I met Kevin and his dad and another former player and mutual friend. After some conversation, an adult beverage and some hors d' oeuvres, Kevin's dad said they needed to get back to Stone Mountain, Georgia. I called for the check and when the server brought it, Kevin's dad snatched it from my hand. He gave it to Kevin with the remark, "I don't see but one millionaire sitting at this table." Now, 26 years afterward, I asked what Kevin misses most about professional football, he answered, "The paychecks."...

Joe Geri, from Pennsylvania, was of Hungarian origin like so many of our football players over the years. His career was interrupted by World War II when he joined the Marines and became a naval loader. He was down in the bowels of a ship at D-Day setting up artillery shells. At the end of the war, he came back to the University of Georgia and continued his education. After he graduated, he was drafted by the Pittsburgh Steelers. Then he was traded to St. Louis where they used to play football and baseball on the same plot of ground, which meant they had to move sod around as the seasons changed. Joe always stayed on the field for the entire game—college or pro. He handled the ball, kicked extra points, played defense—you name it. He did everything except sell popcorn. One time Joe went out to attempt an extra point. He kicked, and the ref raised his arms to indicate that he had made the kick. But, when they looked down, the ball was still laying right off the tee. What had gone over the crossbars was a piece of sod. The coach looked from the side and said, "If it had been a Schlitz beer, he wouldn't have missed it." Joe ultimately was an assistant coach at UT-Chattanooga. He retired to Athens where he and I were friends until his death.

—LEN DAVIS, 64, Athens, Georgia

I played football at a small private high school and didn't get much attention from the big schools coming out. I got a scholarship offer from a Division II school in Missouri and went there to play. I couldn't live with myself without giving Georgia a shot. I always wanted to be a Bulldog. I transferred to Georgia and walked on as a fullback. My first fall I was red-shirted. When Coach Donnan was fired, I thought I had made the biggest mistake of my life. But then, when Coach Richt came in everything worked out. He actually ran a scheme that utilized the fullback more and was better for me.

The first time I ran out of the tunnel at Sanford Stadium, it was amazing There were 90,000 people screaming their heads off. I couldn't hear a thing. Growing up, I had always wanted to do that. The only thing that kept running through my mind was, "Don't fall. Don't fall. Don't fall." I didn't want to be that one guy who fell running through the sign with everybody looking at me.

I loved going to Alabama to play. That was probably the most pumped-up I ever was for a game. When we were on the field for the pre-game, it was an unbelievable atmosphere. We were warming up, then it all went silent, and they started playing "Sweet Home Alabama"

Georgia football was a lifelong dream, that I was very fortunate to be able to live out. It's something a lot of people want to do but very few have the chance. I'm really thankful to God and to my family and Coach Richt to have given me that opportunity. It meant the world to me. I can always look back and say, "I was a part of something special."

—J.T. WALL, 28, personal trainer

I knew Mike Cavan in school, but didn't know him very well. In the last couple of years, we've gotten to be real good friends. It's got nothing to do with Georgia, but we've re-met, and his wife and my wife think the world of each other. We spend a fair amount of time together. He's going to be my guest in an upcoming golf tournament. When I was at Georgia, I had a date to go to a game with Mimi Dubose. Her father was a well respected doctor in Athens. I dated Mimi a little while and she was a neighbor, so I used to go to some of the games with her and her family. My parents watched the games, but they weren't big on getting into all the madness of going. Dr. Dubose always went to the games. I was there with Mimi, and Mike was playing quarterback. He had thrown about five interceptions. Dr. Dubose was this very mild-mannered physician, snow white hair, and a pillar of the community. He'd had about enough of Mike throwing interceptions. I'll never forget, I was sitting next to him, when he stood up and shouted, "Hey, Mike, how about throwing it to somebody with a red shirt on for a change." It was completely out of character for him, but he sure made his point.

> Before Larry Munson moved to Athens, he would stay in the Ramada...

—RICK BEACHAM, 57, Marietta, Georgia

We never did much tailgating when I was in school, of course. As players we had to get ready for the game. But after I left my favorite tailgate was a Georgia-Florida game. We rode the bus down and drank a lot. Once we got to the game, we'd try to sober up and find a place to go to the bathroom. One time we were early, and they wouldn't let us in. I was dying to go to the bathroom, so when I saw the Florida players going into the stadium, I walked in with them. I went to the bathroom in their dressing room and looked around and there was an old friend from Savannah, who had played for Florida when I played and who was coaching down there. He looked at me and said, "Dukes, what are you doing in here?" I said, "I'm scouting, man." They asked me to leave....

Before Larry Munson moved to Athens, he would stay in the Ramada, now the Holiday Inn Express, in Athens. We would get together and talk. He always wanted my projections and my predictions. I'd give them to him, and I'd be about right on the money. He couldn't believe it. I studied the teams. For years, he'd call me wherever I was to ask my opinion. I'd say, "Well Larry, looks like a 7-3 year." "Aw, really!" "Yeah, I don't see how we're going to beat Florida or Auburn or Alabama or LSU," or whoever it was. "You've got to have talent."

—LEROY DUKES, President Emeritus of the Letterman's Club

I graduated from Georgia in 1982. My first job out of college was in Charleston, West Virginia, in television news. My first or second day on the job, somebody in the newsroom—and it was a crowded newsroom—said, "Where did you go to school, again?" I said, "Herschel Walker University." Everybody in the room understood what I was talking about except for one woman, Sherry Solijay, who looked up and said, "Who the hell would name a school that?" Everybody died laughing. She was the one person on the face of the earth who didn't know who Herschel Walker was.

Herschel was, and continues to be, a very special person in the hearts of University of Georgia people. Not only is he an extremely talented and gifted man, he also happens to be a very classy man. He let his playing do his talking for him. He has supported the university through the years, financially and otherwise. I think you have to look far and wide to find a classier man than Herschel Walker.

—MARK KING, 47, Fresno, California

When they had the 100th Anniversary of Georgia Football in 1992, they did a big autograph signing event. Herschel Walker, Kevin Butler, Mo Lewis and all these people were there. Everyone was standing in line for Herschel. I ran around and got all the other autographs and got to talk to Kevin Butler for a while because my brother was a kicker. I met Vince Dooley. Herschel's line went around the stadium. They were trying to pull him away, get him to stop signing autographs because they wanted to start the game. My mom had barely made a dent in the line. There was a kid standing in line with his dad, and he just wanted to see Herschel, so I took him to get a closer look at him. Somebody started to pull Herschel away. I had a 1981 program that I'd saved from a game. When they started pulling him away, everybody rushed toward him to try and get him to sign their stuff. I held up my program, and he just happened to see it and saw that it was one of the old ones from when he played. He grabbed it and signed it. That was the last thing he signed as they were pulling him away. So, I have a 1981 Georgia-Tennessee program with his and Kevin Butler's and Vince Dooley's autographs on it.

—MICHELLE HERITAGE, UGA '93

One time, we caught a 10-pound catfish. A defensive back named Abb Ansley, played on the team. There was never anything out of place on him—his shirt collar was starched—everything was starched, and he was always prim and proper. We cut the head off that catfish and snuck into his room and hung it up in his closet.

—CRAIG HERTWIG, offensive lineman

The reason Northwestern has two directions in their name is they don't know if they're coming or going.

What's the definition of gross sports ignorance?

144 LSU fans

Chapter 6

Ah, A Female Dawg Fan—No Man is Worthy

Ginger Rogers Did Everything Fred Astaire Did and She Did It In High Heels While Going Backward

SOUTHERN HERITAGE

Michelle Heritage

Marriages and bulldogs are made in heaven—so are thunder and lightning. Heritage combined both by tying the knot during Gator Hater week at St. Simons Island in 2005. The Kennesaw native showed her Colorado fiancé the party style of the Bulldog Nation. Heritage, 36, is a vital cog for a wholesale sportswear company near her home in Wheatridge, Colorado. Still a season-ticket holder, she and her husband try to make two home games a year.*

When I was a little girl, my step-grandfather had tickets on the 50-yard line. I would get to go to one game a year with him and my nana. They tailgated behind the business building before the construction there with the same group of people. A red van would show up and play music at the Kappa Alpha house. I would say, "When I grow up, I'm going to go to one of those parties." I thought that was the coolest day. That was in the early eighties, so those were *Herschel days.* My first Georgia memory is watching the national championship game at a party at their house. Before the party, we made signs that read things like, "How About Them Dawgs?" Each of us had a different poster, and we walked up to the house carrying them.

I met my husband, a **COLORADO*** native, in Colorado. He had no collegiate alliance whatsoever. He and I would actually fight over which was better—college football or pro football.

After one Georgia game, I had him convinced. About seven years ago, I took him to Athens when we played Tennessee and beat

---

*In the upper deck at Coors Field in Denver, <u>COLORADO</u> there is a single row of seats all painted purple. They denote that the elevation of that row is exactly one mile high—5,280 feet above sea level.

---

them for the first time in 12 years. That was his first college football game. When the team stormed the field, the stadium was just wild. He never had two thoughts again about pro football being better. I had him hooked.

We were planning our wedding, and I'd always joked that I wanted to get married on the 50-yard line, at halftime with the band playing and Uga escorting me down the field. Of course, I was not serious about any of that, but I had always wanted a 'tailgate wedding.' Everybody tailgates—we get married—we all go to the game and have a great day. He wasn't too up for that. The other thing we always talked about was having a beach wedding.

> I would say, "When I grow up, I'm going to go to one of those parties."

It finally occurred to me, less than a year from the date, that I could have both. We talked about doing it at St. Simons on Georgia-Florida weekend. We weren't sure we'd be able to get a place to stay or have people come in because it's so crazy down there. We went down on Thanksgiving 2004, the year before our wedding and found the perfect place.

Before we contacted any real estate company about rentals, we were walking down the beach, and we saw this house that looks like a barn. I was joking about how perfect it would be. It turned out to be the only house available on the beach. We got that place, which had a gigantic back yard for us to have the reception. We found this incredible house for his family and we were able to get the Quality Inn to set aside rooms for guests that weekend.

I met most of my friends in Colorado through the alumni group. We're known as the Georgia Girls. All my Georgia Girls came in and wore red and black for the wedding. We were able to scrounge up enough tickets so that anyone who wanted to go was able to go to the game the next day. The wedding ceremony was Friday night at the Gazebo. Then, everybody came back to the barn for a big outdoor reception. Our next-door temporary neighbors—they were from Vidalia who come to St. Simons every year—started helping us. They came over to the reception and danced and partied with us. They even bought us a wedding present. We had just met them two days before. Everything was red and black and silver without being overtly Georgia. My husband had 18 mini cakes done in Georgia colors. Every couple could have their own cake. It was grab and go instead of having to slice cake. We had red, black and silver brownies. It was a subtle-Georgia theme.

> My world stops at the end of August, and it's all about Georgia football.

During the sunset ceremony at the Gazebo, people walked by, but everybody was very respectful when they saw what was going on. Some people stopped by to congratulate us or yell, "Go Dawgs!" It was real casual, a huge party, which is exactly what we wanted.

The next day, we went down to the game with our wedding leftovers for tailgating. My friend, Lisa, who coordinates my Georgia group in Colorado, scored some amazing parking passes. We were in the main parking lot. We met a guy we call "Dawg Man," the one who always paints bulldogs on his car. We had our picture taken with him. We saw all these people walking around with bulldogs, and we took our pictures with all of them. We had an absolute blast.

Georgia football is my life. My world stops at the end of August, and it's all about Georgia football. It has brought me most of my friends in Colorado. But the biggest thing for me is bonding with my dad. If there's news about Georgia football, we're on the phone immediately with each other. On a game-day Saturday, we'll talk five or six times. That's our bonding. He calls me from the stadium so I can listen to things. He'll call me after a touchdown and let me hear the crowd. The most important things to me are the relationships in my life, especially, with my dad.

VINCE DOOLEY STRUCK OIL ONE DAY... AT THE ALTAR

Barbara Dooley

Dooley is the wife of Vince Dooley, one of the most notable coaches in the history of college football. The Dooleys, especially Barbara, play an active role in the University community. They are the iconic Southern couple: gracious, generous, humble and passionate. They still live in Athens.

Forty-something years ago, when Vince and I first came to the University of Georgia, the stadium wasn't anything like the stadium is now. It was much smaller. I can remember thinking how awesome it was to see the students back then, sitting on top of the roofs of buildings to look at the game, so they wouldn't have to pay to get in. The ones who were in the stadium wore coats and ties. We dressed up back then to go to a game. The whole atmosphere was quite different. It was not as rowdy as it is today. Of course, there weren't as many people. Georgia had not been winning. The excitement and enthusiasm really didn't pick up until about the third or fourth game. Then, it was like the Georgia students caught on fire. They've come a long way.

I was pretty wild back then—young and very protective of my husband. I remember taking my young children to the games. All the coach's wives sat in one section together. There was a man near us going nuts, saying all sorts of bad words about my husband, about the defensive coordinator, about the offensive coordinator, about the players. I had asked him twice to behave. And, he didn't. So, I picked up my Coca-Cola and dumped it on his head. I had to have two men hold him off of me. I thought he was going to kill me. He was drunk, but we got him out of the stands, and he never got tickets again. Don't mess with me when you start talking about our staff and my husband.

> So, I picked up my Coca-Cola and dumped it on his head.

There were a lot of wonderful, exciting games in Jacksonville. I'm not good with scores and years, but we were killing Florida one year in the late sixties. It was 50-something to nothing. It was pouring down rain. I had on a white knit dress—that was the fad back then—and a red raincoat. By the time the game was over, my dress had turned pink from the red raincoat and had grown. The wetter it got, the longer it got. It was like an evening dress by the time the game ended. But we didn't care. We were beating Florida terribly, and it didn't matter if it rained or not.

Going into the national championship game is indescribable. We were so nervous before the game. We had our family prayers. Of course, we always prayed to win. We asked the Lord to let us win that game. As we got down to the final seconds of the game, I grabbed all the kids, and we were holding hands. I was praying as hard as I could. I can remember when that final whistle blew, and it was over, I've never seen anything to equal the excitement. People mobbed down on the field to the point that it was almost scary. The whole field was covered in red and black. But, I don't think anybody cared, because we did it. We beat Notre Dame.

I didn't go to many of the out-of-town games when my children were little. I stayed at home, but I always went to the Florida game. Vince did not let the wives travel with the husbands, so we traveled separately. But, he would give us a ride to the airport on the team buses. The first Florida game I went to, I had never seen Larry Munson in person. Here was this guy with a crew cut on the bus with us. He introduced himself, and I still had no clue who he was. I said, "Well, do you come to all the games?" He said, "What?" I said, "Do you come to all the games?" I thought Vince was going to pass out. How stupid can you be! I think Larry and I bonded at that moment.

Georgia football has been my whole life. The children were wrapped up in Georgia football. The players were like my children. Their families were like my families. Players like Billy Payne and Frank Ross and Kirby Moore and Nixon Robinson—there are just so many. I hate to name names, because then I'm going to leave somebody out.

When Billy Payne was trying to get the **OLYMPICS*** to Atlanta, his wife dressed up in an outfit with a long, black wig and a real tight shirt and skirt, real high heels. He was on the stage talking, and she *slinked* up. He had no idea who she was. He became a nervous wreck....

Frank Ross was the captain of the 1980 team. We hired a few of the players to wash windows. They were so good looking that I didn't get a thing done all day but walk around watching them wash windows.

*The 1996 Atlanta OLYMPICS had more journalists than athletes. There were 10,000 athletes and 15,000 reporters.

IF YOU WANT BREAKFAST IN BED— SLEEP IN THE KITCHEN

Every so often I take a group of about 35 students and student athletes as part of a course on Housing and Consumer Policy in Action to Washington, D.C. The trip is preceded by classroom preparation. In Washington we do tours and lectures and conclude with visits to individual congressional offices. It's a wonderful experience for these students. Several years ago we were in the midst of a tour of the U.S. Capitol building and the entire group was walking down one of those huge marble staircases where the steps are worn from the feet of millions of tourists and politicians over the years. As the group walked down the steps I heard a thud, unmistakably the sound of a person falling down on the stairs. I pushed my way through the group to find that the person who fell was a scholarship football player, Terrell Davis. My mind raced as I pictured facing Coach Goff and explaining how one of his players went with my class to Washington only to return just before football season with a broken leg! Today, it's even worse! I relive that scene in my dreams, only this time he's more than a student athlete. He's a **SUPER BOWL*** MVP!!!

> I heard a thud, unmistakably the sound of a person falling down on the stairs.

After Coach Donnan left, we were flying back from the Oahu Bowl in Hawaii. It was a subdued trip because of the uncertainty of this sudden loss of leadership. I was on the Athletic Board at the time and during the flight I was notified that the next day I was to come to a meeting with the Executive Committee in the fifth floor conference room of the Georgia Center. When I arrived at the meeting the Executive Board was already there. President Adams and Vince Dooley were about to introduce the new head

*Each **SUPER BOWL** player gets two free tickets and can buy 13 more at face value.

football coach, Mark Richt. After a few words of introduction, Mark Richt began to speak. He was an articulate and serious young man as he spoke of his goals for the program. He spoke of education as a primary goal. He emphasized the importance of student athletes taking advantage of this wonderful opportunity to learn and to get a degree. He said his objective was to get all of his football players to graduate. I felt compelled to ask a question. "Are you going to win?" Everyone laughed and President Adams said, "and that's coming from one of our academic members!" Hey, I'm also a huge Bulldog fan! I wanted to know....

Terrell Davis was a wonderful student. I can still see him sitting where he usually sat in the classroom. He did like to sleep a lot, but he was also interested in graduating. It was important to him to finish. He promised me that he would come back and go through the ceremony. We had a college ceremony and then a university ceremony. I will never forget looking back—he'd gone on, he was in Denver then, and had to come back to go through the ceremonies. He said, "I promised I'd be here."

Robert Edwards had a major injury in Hawaii. They were playing some kind of game on the sand and his foot slipped and he injured his leg. I remember him coming to Dawson Hall after he was injured, and he said, "I am going to play again." No one believed him. But he's playing in Canada right now.

The memory I have about Hines Ward is of him sitting by the windows in a large lecture room. He, too, was determined to graduate because his mother had worked so hard for him to be in school. She had three jobs when he was growing up. He really wanted to finish his degree before he went on. He finished the degree as an Academic All-American with above a 3.0 grade average. I also remember during the Olympics he told me he'd met somebody from his home country, Korea. He had not been there before as an adult. He was very proud to be from Korea and proud of his heritage. He met this girl, from Korea, during the Olympics, and he wrote me an email telling me all about that.

—ANNE SWEANEY, Executive Committee member,
University Athletic Board

Georgia football has had a big impact on me. I've been developing a tool for football teams to scout their opponents. It's one of the things I'm pretty passionate about.

My love of football comes from my dad. My mom didn't like football. She always wanted to go shopping. My dad would talk me into staying with him and watching the Georgia game. He taught me about football. We watched both college and professional football. We still watch football games together. It's nice to have that common interest.

> The Georgia 101 women's camp is fabulous.

I grew up in a rural northwest Georgia town outside of Chattanooga called Flintstone. In rural areas, football is such an important part of the social life. When you're in high school, that's what you do every Friday night—you go to football games. It's social, not just about the sport. I go into a depression in January after football season is over. I can't wait until the season kicks off, and we get to have Georgia football again.

The Georgia 101 women's camp is fabulous. One of my friends asked me to go last year, so I signed up. I think, for a woman, I know quite a bit about football, but I'm trying to learn more, especially because we've been developing this software tool for football. I thought it would be good. I thought they were probably going to cover the basics, and it would be real rudimentary...but it wasn't. In fact, they started talking about game strategy. They showed us video clips. They talked about the different position coaches. They got us out on the field doing drills. We got to tour the locker room and the training room, which were really neat and very nice. We got to watch motivational tapes and hear Mark Richt speak. It was fabulous. They twitched it up a little bit this year. You could pick offense or defense so there was more in-depth focus. We got in and looked at their plays and formations. I was on defense and really took a deeper dive. We got out on the field and didn't just do drills. We actually wound up in some of those formations, defensive formations, and worked on the field, too.

I love football so that's why I go. They get over 500 women who want to do this, and they turn a lot of women away because there isn't room for them all. I'm amazed that there are that many women who have that level of interest.

Coach Martinez is the defensive coordinator. He's used to getting in players' faces. He was joking with us and getting in our faces, and I don't know if he really "gets" Southern women, but no matter what we do, we're going to have our makeup and our jewelry on. He's got these women who look like they're ready to go to the Junior League, and they're on the field in practice jerseys. He got in some woman's face, and she got all teary-eyed. I just got back in his face when he got in my

> "Ladies, there's no crying in football."

face. This year, he told us right off the bat, "Ladies, there's no crying in football." Right up front, we knew what the expectation was. A few of the women were running out on the field with their cameras around their necks. He said, "Get those cameras off the field. You're out here to do drills. You're not out here to take pictures." I'm going to go back next year. I love defense, but I need to learn more about offense so I think I'll be on offense, next year. The camp lasts a whole day. It starts about 8:30 in the morning and goes until six in the evening.

Last year Coach Richt and his wife, Katharyn spoke at the lunch we had. This year, he was getting ready to head out on a mission trip, so he came to the training room and spent 15-20 minutes with us and gave us a quick talk and answered questions. The commitment they make to this is really interesting and very much appreciated....

I'm a Gator Hater, and Florida was here in Atlanta for the basketball championships. I was out walking my dog when these Florida guys were going by in their truck with their flags flying. They stopped and asked directions. I said, "I'd like to help y'all. I'm so sorry y'all are lost, but you're the enemy. You're Florida fans, and I'm a Georgia Bulldog—I really can't help you out today." In the end, I made them bark, and then I helped them out.

Georgia football has had a big impact on my life. In fact, my passion for football has become a business interest. No matter where I've lived in the country, I try to pick up a Georgia game and follow the Dawgs. It's something that just doesn't leave you.

Once you're part of the Bulldog Nation, you're always part of the Bulldog Nation no matter where you're living.
—DIANE BLOODWORTH, UGA '82, President of Scouting Pros, Atlanta, Georgia

I'm a nut for bulldogs. I mean, I'm a nut for the breed, and I am also a nut for Georgia Bulldogs. Shortly after my bulldog, Higgins, died, I was walking with a friend and spotted a bulldog wandering around the neighborhood by himself. That's really rare because these dogs are expensive. I said to my friend, "My God, there's a bulldog!" My Higgins was dead, and my heart was going thumpety-thump. I said, "I've got to rescue this bulldog." She said, "Pat, you can't have that bulldog. You know that bulldog belongs to someone." I said, "No, he doesn't. He's off by himself. Poor, precious puppy." She said, "Pat, you can't keep that bulldog. He belongs to somebody." We began canvassing the neighborhood in Dunwoody, Georgia. We soon found a gentleman out looking for his bulldog, Silver Britches. He said the bulldog was from Sonny Seiler's line of Georgia bulldogs. As I talked to his owner, he told me that Britches, as he called him, had substituted for Uga IV when the dog had injured his leg jumping off a motel bed. The Georgia bulldog travels with the team in Mr. Seiler's red car with the license plate, Uga IV. When the dog was injured, Britches was asked to step in because he was out of the same litter as Uga IV, but he was not the purest white—he was more of a silver color and that's why he was named Silver Britches. I told the man, "Any time you need a babysitter for this dog, please call me. I will be happy to baby-sit Silver Britches because my bulldog is gone, and I haven't replaced him." When Britches walked into my house I could tell he wasn't just a pet. Britches was regal. He was used to being served. He walked in like he owned the place. And, he did, anytime I baby sat him. So, I was the surrogate babysitter for Silver Britches, who I thought was the surrogate for Uga IV through five Georgia games when Uga IV was out. I was recently informed that Silver Britches was not the surrogate for Uga IV, Otto was! So what, it was fun while the story lasted but I still love English bulldogs and, of course, Georgia Bulldogs.

I love Georgia football. I do not go anywhere in the fall during football season. In fact, my husband, Harry, and I are going to celebrate our 50th anniversary in Italy. My brother keeps telling me that October is the best time to go to Italy, but I say, "Uh-uh, the Dawgs play in October. I'm not going to be in Italy, while my Bulldogs play." He thinks that's the funniest thing. Trust me, we're going in April cause the Dawgs don't play in the springtime.

—PAT GEISINGER, 70, Roswell, Georgia

For the last 10 years, I was director of the J.W. Fanning Institute for Leadership. We had a faculty member, Susan Taylor, who was an avid Georgia Tech fan, even though she got her paychecks from the University of Georgia. Although we tried, we were never able to convert her to being a Bulldogs fan. Our computer technician, Jamie, was a rabid Georgia Bulldog. He was so rabid, in fact, he had a vanity tag on his vehicle that read 'THWGT,' which stood for To Hell with Georgia Tech. Those two went at each other constantly whenever we played Georgia Tech.

One year when Georgia won, Jamie came to work early on Monday morning. He went into Susan's office which was loaded with Georgia Tech memorabilia. One of her prize possessions was Buzz, the Georgia Tech mascot, a big stuffed Yellow Jacket. Jamie strung Buzz up in effigy with a computer cord and tied a University of Georgia bandana around its neck. He got on her computer and downloaded the Georgia fight song and turned the volume up as loud as it would go. He changed her screensaver to Uga kicking the Georgia Tech Yellow Jacket's butt across the screen. Finally he turned every bit of her Georgia Tech memorabilia face down.

We all heard several choice words when she turned the light on and saw Buzz hanging in effigy. Then, she turned her computer on. Down the hall blasted the Georgia fight song. Then, she logged on and the Uga screensaver came on. After lunch, Jamie programmed the computer to download Larry Munson's calling of a favorite play of his. Unfortunately, Susan was computer savvy enough to take all of that off the computer herself without relying on Jamie.

—MELBA COOPER, Bishop, Georgia; retired faculty member

My grandfather went to Georgia during prohibition. They would sneak bootleg liquor into the football games in Sanford Stadium. One time they dropped the bottle, and it broke! So that nobody would know they had alcohol, they set fire to it.

I'm from Atlanta originally. My dad went to Tech. When I went to Georgia, he used to make fun of me. I teased him back by calling his school the "North Avenue Trade School".

When I was in school, I went to all the games. I remember the smell of bourbon in the stadium. We always used to wear dresses to games. I know they are doing that again now. I started school in 1969, but by '70, we were wearing jeans to the games. My first year, we would dress up, and go to the fraternity house for lunch and then go to the game, and it was such a big deal.

The first time we played Tennessee when I was a student a train pulled up at the end of the stadium that was still open. All of a sudden, this sea of orange poured off the train and filled up parts of Sanford Stadium. After the game, they got back onto the train and off they went. I'm sure that doesn't happen any more.

It's hard to be a Georgia fan and live up here in **BIG 10*** country, where the only team there is or ever has been is Ohio State. But then, the Gators who are an SEC team, stomped them in the 2007 BCS Bowl. I actually rooted for Ohio State. I wanted them to put the Gators in their place. But, secretly I wanted the SEC to whip up on the Big Ten.

—<u>CAROLINE CLABAUGH</u>, UGA '73, Columbus, Ohio

*The late Randy Walker, head coach at Northwestern from 1999-2005, is the only coach to beat every <u>BIG 10</u> team. When he was head coach at Miami (Ohio), his team beat Northwestern.

Chapter 7

On the Road Again

Today We Ride

SOME SAY THAT YOU CAN MARRY A GATOR FAN, YET STILL GO ON TO LEAD A NORMAL AND PRODUCTIVE LIFE

Rich Ciordia

Ciordia is an anesthesiologist from Pensacola, Florida. He is 62 years old, but during football season he thinks he is still 25. He married his wife Paige even though she was a Florida fan.

In 1982, five or six of us made the four-hour trip from Pensacola to Auburn for the game. We'd had a little bit to drink. We found our seats, the absolute worst seats in the stadium. They were up against a brick wall. The seat was about eight inches wide. We had people sitting right in front of us. We couldn't lean back because of the brick wall. We were complaining about the bad seats, when we noticed this knock-down gorgeous girl coming up the stadium steps. She walked into our row, looked at her ticket and sat down right next to me. My buddy and I had been upset about those seats and suddenly he jumped up and yelled, "Great seats!"...

Another time, at the Sugar Bowl, which had been relocated to the Georgia Dome after Katrina, I was sitting next to this very attractive lady, who was about 45 years old. About halfway through the second quarter, she nudged me in the side and said, "This guy over here's really not my husband. He's my ex-husband. We've been buying these tickets for a long time, and I don't care who I'm sitting with, I'm using these seats." We talked through the game. At the end she said to my friend and me, "How are y'all getting home?" We said, "We don't know." She said, "Well, I'll give you a ride to your hotel if you need one." We thought that sounded pretty good. We walked her to her car. She took us back to our hotel and dropped us off.

The next year, I went to the Georgia-South Carolina game in Columbia, South Carolina. As I walked out of the stadium this big dude walked up to me. He tapped me on the back and said, "Aren't you the guy who took my ex-wife home from the Sugar Bowl?" I said, "Wait a minute. She took me home. I didn't take her home." I don't talk to women at games anymore!

One year, as I was walking out of the Georgia-Florida game, there was a young girl in front of me, who had on an Al Gore button. Florida had won the game and she was berating Georgia and rubbing it in. I said, "You're a two-time loser. You're a Democrat and a Florida Gator." We started exchanging barbs, and I said, "Where are you from, honey?" She said, "I'm from Pensacola, Florida." I said, "Pensacola, Florida. What's your name?" She told me her name, and I said, "You're so and so's daughter aren't you?" She said, "Yes." I said, "I was there when you were born. I'm the first man to ever see you naked." That shut her up. I'm an anesthesiologist. I gave her mother a spinal when she had a C-section. What a coincidence to run into this girl....

> We were complaining about the bad seats, when we noticed this knock-down gorgeous girl coming up the stadium steps.

TENNIS WOULD BE MORE FUN WITHOUT A NET

Hill Griffin

Griffin, 67, is a dentist living in Atlanta. He was a member of Sigma Chi fraternity and graduated from Georgia in 1962. He also played tennis for Dan McGill, the famous University of Georgia coach, and won the SEC singles title in 1962.

At a Georgia-Tennessee football game in Knoxville, I had a double-sided sign. One side read, "Nothing sucks like a big orange." The other side read, "Red necks turn orange in the fall." Going into the stadium, I walked up the aisle between the Georgia and the Tennessee sections. One side cheered the sign; the other side booed. The game was Herschel Walker's coming-out party which we won in a major upset. Most of the Georgia contingency was still sitting there late. The Tennessee people had filed out. I heard this big, deep voice behind me, "You come inside here and insult us like that. I'm going to come down there and whip your ass." The guy looked to be about 6'8" and 300 pounds of rippling muscles. He had overalls on, no shirt, and he was red-eyed drunk. I said, "We're just having a little collegiate fun." He said, "I don't care. I'm going to come down there and stomp your ass." I'm looked at him. He was so big, so strong; I couldn't have hurt him with a baseball bat. I was just about to run, figuring he was too drunk to run after me, when my date said, "Does that mean it's every man for himself?" I said, "Yeah, but he's not after you; he's after me, and I'm sure as heck not going to fight him." A few of his buddies talked to him and peace was made. He walked down, shouting curse words at me as he walked by. I put my head down and thought, "Oh God, don't let him come to me." Nothing happened, but it was a very frightening experience. I rolled the sign up, hid it under my arm and let this guy get out of the way, before I left the stadium. I have since married my date....

My junior year, we were coming back from playing in the SEC tennis tournament. We had driven in two separate cars. We didn't have vans or school vehicles. I rode with one of the guys, and Coach Dan Magill had his big red station wagon. Dan had a few beers, as did some of the people not driving. We stopped in Dublin, Georgia, to get gas. We filled up and drove off. As we got on the highway, the police

> He had overalls on, no shirt, and he was red-eyed drunk.

pulled us over. We didn't know what in the world for. They claimed that we had driven off without paying for the gas. We had paid for our gas, but apparently the people in McGill's vehicle did not. Soon, here came the big red station wagon with McGill and my other teammates. McGill's face was red from the sun and the beer, and we were afraid he was going to stop and get us all in even more trouble. But they circled the incident two or three times and drove off, thank goodness. About that time, the police heard from a girl back at the filling station and said to us, "There's no problem here." But, he took us to jail anyway. They finally realized we were pretty good college kids, we didn't look menacing. My grandfather who had been an upstanding gentleman farmer and intelligent man happened to live about 15-20 miles from there, and they remembered him. He had just died. When I started telling them I had relatives in the Dublin area, they said, "Okay, y'all go on." We got out of it, but it was a harrowing few minutes for a bunch of college kids who were happy to get out of Dublin....

I've been to all the SEC stadiums. I went to Vaught-Hemingway Stadium at Ole Miss. Their big deal is The Grove. We were able to do pre-game and post-game tailgating in The Grove. We felt very fortunate to get to do that. We went to Mississippi State, to their stadium in Starkville and were surprised at how small it was. I went to Arkansas on a charter flight, a big 727, from Atlanta to Fayetteville. We got there and we had our Georgia buttons on and walked around the town and visited the campus. We were amazed at the number of people who came and asked, "Were y'all on that big plane that landed a while ago?" That was the biggest plane they'd ever seen. I know the runway was barely big enough. We were the talk of the town because of the size of the plane we flew in on.

> I would classify myself as the eternal sophomore.

I never will forget, not only did we have a police escort to take the buses in, but they stopped traffic for us through the intersections. And, we weren't even with the team. We were just fans. They treated us like we were something special. We weren't, but they thought we were, and that made it nice.

I would classify myself as the eternal sophomore. I get excited and nervous on Friday nights before a game. It's not life or death, but it's fun to have something to root for. Being a tennis player, and still playing a lot of tennis, I'm very competitive, and it's another type of competition, pulling for the team.

I once asked Vince Dooley if he ever looked at the odds in the paper, and he said, "No. I did once. We were favored to beat some team by two points. We beat this team by two points, and I figured they knew something I didn't know. I've never looked at the odds since then."

TAILGREAT

Jarrell Greene

Greene, 59, has a family-owned water-well contracting business and lives in Gray, Georgia. He graduated from UGA in 1974.

A couple of friends and I go to all the Georgia football games, home and away. I haven't missed a game in 22 years. We tailgate before the games. We enjoy doing that. We always rank our tailgates and we rank our weekends.

We flew to Oxford, Mississippi, several years ago to a Georgia-Ole Miss game. After the game we went to one of the clubs in town. A lot of college kids were there and everybody was having a good time. They had a real good band, The Memphis Icebreakers, that played good old music that all of us grew up with. We got to enjoying the spirits and the occasion a whole lot. I looked up at one moment, and my buddy was pulling two tables together. I wondered what in the world he was doing. The next thing I knew—he took one arm and raked the glasses, the ketchup, and the plates onto the floor. Then, some college coed got up on the table dancing. Following the Dawgs is like sex: when it's good, it's really good...and when it's bad, it's still good...

> "Man, why did you have your wedding on a football game day?"

For as many games as I've been to, I missed Herschel Walker's debut because of a wedding. I was going. I had tickets. My cousin decided he would set his wedding day on that day, and I said something to him about it. We had almost lived together at one time. I said, "Man, why did you have your wedding on a football game day?" He said, "Well, don't come then." I knew right then I just needed to be quiet and go to the wedding....

I went to the Sugar Bowl in '82 when **PENN STATE*** beat us. We flew on a private plane to New Orleans. Left Macon early that morning. As soon as we pulled off the runway, we couldn't see the ground, and we didn't see the ground again until just before we touched down. It was a bad-weather day. I've never been any more mad at Vince Dooley than I was that day. Coach Dooley had a philosophy. It worked, and he won a lot of ball games with it, but not that day. He insisted on using Herschel Walker as his whole offense, and he didn't care what anybody said. He didn't care what anybody did to counteract that. They shut us down pretty well. I was disappointed in the strategy surrounding the football game. But, that was Coach Dooley. I can't fault him too much. We were No. 1 in the nation. We would have finished No. 1 again if we'd won that game—for the second national championship in three years, but we didn't.

My favorite part of Georgia football is really not football—it's the activity surrounding football games. One year three of us went to Lexington, to the University of Kentucky game. We didn't have much to do before the game, so we headed to the stadium early. When I say 'early,' I mean 'early.' We got there at eleven o'clock in the morning for a seven o'clock kickoff. There was almost nobody around in this big open parking lot. We spotted a Georgia flag and decided to park by it. As it turned out, they were Georgia fans from Georgia, but they were also with a group of Kentucky fans. Some of the Kentucky people lived in Georgia, and they all got together and went back to Kentucky for the football game and a nice fun weekend. We were sitting on the back of our car talking. We had a boom box and were playing some music. The Kentucky crowd started growing. Then, more Georgia fans started coming around. Before we knew it, there was a fairly significant group of people who knew each other or had common connections. My

---

*A Nittany Lion, a Cougar and a Puma are the same animal...Joe Paterno's son, Jay, was a backup quarterback for <u>PENN STATE</u> '86-'89.

two buddies and I didn't know any of them. Before too long one of the Kentucky guys came over and said, "Look, what y'all need to do is turn your car around so we can listen to y'alls music, and y'all just tailgate with us the rest of the day. That was 20 or 25 years ago. To this day, when we go to Kentucky, we meet that crowd and we have parties at night. We go out to dinner and have a good social weekend—with the same group of people we met that first day in the parking lot....

We've made a lot of good friends going to games. Now when we go to away games, we have friends, and we tailgate with them. When they come to Georgia, they tailgate with us. I tell everybody in the world—and some people don't like it this way—"Look, that guy's just like me. He just wears a different color shirt on Saturdays than I do." He's the same kind of person I am. He just dresses up different than I do. I get along with *most* of our visiting teams' fans pretty well. There are a few....I haven't found any Florida fans I like yet.

> My favorite part of Georgia football is really not football—it's the activity surrounding football games.

I've only been to LSU three or four times. I've talked to people who like to go to LSU. We've had success there, but their fans are a bit aggressive. From the time you get there on Thursday or Friday afternoon, you get cussed out walking down the sidewalk. They'll get in your face over at the stadium. You walk to the stadium and they throw little dog biscuits down around your feet. Florida did that when we went to Gainesville. I hope I never have to go back to Gainesville, Florida again. I can stomach the LSU rivalry because we don't play them every year. If we played them every year, I probably wouldn't like LSU at all....

We were coming back from an LSU football game one weekend. We had a TV in the car and were watching the World Series. We were about 50 miles from home, and it was dark—eight or nine o'clock on Sunday night. It had been a long weekend, and we were having a few beers watching baseball coming home. All of a sudden, something happened to the car, a belt broke or something. We had to pull over to the side of the road in a rural area. We wondered what we were going to do. In a few minutes, a state patrolman came by. He pulled off and asked us what was wrong. We told him we had a problem. My wife's sister lived in a small town about 10 miles ahead. He offered to give us a ride there. I jumped in the car with him and left my two buddies. He said he knew somebody in town who would help me out. Then, he dropped me at her house, turned around and went back to my two buddies. He said to them, "I had to lock your friend up." They said, "What?" He said, "Well, he was DUI." Then he left. They didn't know what to do. I didn't know anything about this. I got my brother-in-law's car and drove back out to get them. Until I drove up, they thought I was locked up in jail....

The last time we went to Alabama, it may have been the hottest football game I've ever been to in my life. We got there early, parked by 7:00 a.m. for a late afternoon game. We were at a shady place on campus. We had our group, a good crowd. We had gotten there so early we couldn't go by the great rib place, Dreamland Barbecue. We got to having a good time then everybody said, "Heck, let's go to Dreamland and pick up some barbecue ribs and bring them back to our tailgate." My daughter and my niece said they would take a cab and go get it. They were walking down the sidewalk. They turned the corner and, as they did, they almost ran into Herschel Walker. He was on his way to interview at "College Gameday." My daughter is almost as big a Georgia football fan as I am and my niece is the same. They were beside themselves and acted real teenage-girlish, gushing over "Herschel Walker!" They made it to Dreamland, but it was several hours before they could get back because of the wait once they got there, and the cab ride back, which took forever with the traffic.

I enjoy beating Tech because it's an in-state rival. You go head-to-head, year-round, all the time. Tech is not a big deal...until it's the Tech game. They're not in our conference. They don't have any impact on us in our conference race. Our conference race is what we're trying to win—*until* the last game of the year. Conference or not, Tech's the team you want to beat. When the week of that game comes up, that's the most important game of the year. Georgia-Florida is out the door. Georgia-Auburn is behind us. All the other rivals—Tennessee, who we need to beat in order to win the conference, they're behind us. There seems to be, from my perspective, a tad of arrogance from Tech fans: They are smarter than Georgia fans; they are better than Georgia fans, whatever they say, look at the record. We've won quite a few more football games than they've won. So, whatever else they think is okay with me...I'm keeping score.

> I've got hundreds of friends that I wouldn't have met if I hadn't gone to Georgia football games.

Georgia football means a lot to me. I'll do anything it takes to go. I'm a lot older, and it's a lot more physically demanding on me to go to a game and get there at 7 o'clock in the morning and not leave until two hours after the game's over with, whenever that is. But, I'm more than willing to pay the price to go. I've enjoyed it since the early 1960s. I get emails daily from friends of mine—somebody doing the countdown—52 days, 51 days....I've got hundreds of friends that I wouldn't have met if I hadn't gone to Georgia football games.

'TIS BETTER TO TRAVEL WELL THAN TO ARRIVE FIRST

Harvey Elerson

Elerson, 49, a dentist, lives in Statesboro, Georgia. He grew up in Waycross and graduated from UGA in 1980. He has traveled for over ten years in his RV to attend away games.

W e would take our motor home to the Georgia-Florida game on Monday night so we could get a spot in the motor coach parking area there. We would stay there until the next Sunday. It was like a little city there where people would put their RVs together. There would be bands out there playing. It was pretty crazy.

In 1985, Florida was ranked #1. We went in there, and everybody thought we were going to get killed. A friend of mine went down there with no ticket. It was in the old Gator Bowl. My uncle and I went in and told him where we were going to be sitting. He circled the stadium a couple of times. The old ticket takers used to stand in the space behind the wall. He waited until one of them got busy and shot in behind him and came up and sat with us. Every time we'd mix a drink, Worley or Henderson would score a touchdown. We'd have our drink, and have to start over.

After the game, the Georgia fans stormed the field. That was the last time anybody got on that field. After that, they started putting the horses out. We were on the field chanting, "four whole days," because that's how long Florida was ranked #1. That was a good one.

My freshman year was '76, when we beat Alabama 21-0 in Athens, and everybody thought they were going to kill us. That's the wildest I've ever seen Athens. I lived in Russell Hall. On Friday night before the game that area between Russell and Brumby, at three-thirty in the morning, was like it was one o'clock in the afternoon. Everybody was so jacked up for the game. The Alabama team stayed at the Holiday Inn. That's probably the last time they'll make that mistake. People were driving by all night long blowing their horns.

After the game, they shut Milledge Avenue down all the way to Lumpkin. Some semis were stuck in there and people were up on top of them. The fraternities—who could have their kegs out on their front lawns—were giving the truck drivers cups of beer and climbing up on top of the trucks....

> We were on the field chanting, "four whole days," because that's how long Florida was ranked #1.

My freshman year I didn't get tickets to the Florida game but went to Jacksonville anyway. There was a chain-link fence all the way around the stadium. This little guy, about eight years old, comes up to me. He wants to sell me a pass-out for eight bucks. With a pass-out he told me I could go in and out. I could mix a drink before going back in. I was worried that it was a scam. I grabbed him by the back of his shirt collar and walked up to the gate. When they took that pass-out and let me in, I let him go. He scurried on down the fence. As I was walking in, I saw him going over again. He was going to get him another one to sell. That's probably the closest I've come to not getting a ticket—having to buy a pass-out. This little kid was an entrepreneur. He was going in, getting pass-outs, coming out, selling them, and then going back in...to do it all over again....

When my son, Trey, was a year old, we took him over—like everybody else—to have his picture made with Uga. We sat him up on the table and just as they snapped the picture, Uga's long tongue licked the side of my son's face. The photographer got our name. He didn't realize at the time, and neither did I, what kind of picture he had. They put it on the front page of the Athens paper that year....

The Annual Georgia Senior Gala included a silent auction. I was high bidder on a trip with the team to Auburn in 2002 and again

> VanHalanger said, "Breakfast is from eight to ten, and Big Max eats *from eight to ten.*"

on a trip to Tennessee in 2003. When we traveled with the team to the Auburn game, we ate meals with the coaches and the team. Each dinner was with different coaches. Most of the meals were structured where the seniors get their food, then the juniors, then coaches and everybody, but breakfast was open that morning from 8 to 10. We sat down with Coach VanHalanger. We were eating and talking. Big Max Jean-Gilles was sitting at another table with a big old plate of food. He got up and got another one and another one. VanHalanger said, "Breakfast is from eight to ten, and Big Max eats *from eight to ten.*"

Coach Richt is really a laid-back guy. He expects a lot of his players, and if they don't produce, he lets them know. They understand and respect him for it. They know what he wants. He doesn't yell or carry on like a lot of coaches do. I have heard him in the locker room. We were on the sidelines for the Arkansas game when Eddie Brown blew his knee out. At halftime, I heard Coach Richt get a little fired up. He told them they were making Arkansas look like an NFL team. They came out for second half and got a little more motivated. He's not a screamer or a hollerer—players respect him because they trust him. That's the biggest thing. He tells them something and they know that's the way it's going to be.

HE THOUGHT SHE'D NEVER SHUT UP

Frank H. McTeer, Jr.

Frank McTeer, 53, a longtime Bulldog fan, operates Low Country Catering in Savannah, Georgia. He and his wife Elizabeth and their children, Angus and Olivia, live in Savannah.

In 1972, when I was a junior in high school some friends and I got free tickets to the Georgia-Tennessee game. I hit the road out of Savannah with my best friend and our dates to watch Georgia play in Knoxville.

On the way up Sarah, the girl I was with, said, "Oh my goodness, my jaw is stuck wide open." I said, "What?" She said, "Well, I've got these loose muscles, and sometimes my jaw sticks wide open and I can't close it." I thought, "Boy, this is something else." She managed to close it that time.

The next day we went to the game and at halftime the two girls went to the ladies' room. Katherine, my friend's date, came out screaming that Sarah's jaw got stuck again while they were in the bathroom. Sarah came out and, sure enough, her jaw was stuck. Her mouth was open as wide as it could get. She could barely talk, and we could hardly understand her. She could not close her mouth.

> ...sure enough, her jaw was stuck. Her mouth was open as wide as it could get.

We ran from the clubhouse level down every level, which was a pretty good ways, and kept running into security guards who wanted to know why we needed the ambulance. I said, "Well, look at her." We got in the ambulance, and they took us to St. Mary's Catholic Hospital.

Sarah, being only 16, couldn't sign a release for the injection she needed to relax the muscles to let her jaw close. We tried calling her parents, and we couldn't get them. This was the first time I'd ever been out with this girl. I didn't know much about her.

Finally at three o'clock, the shift changed at the hospital. An Oriental doctor came in and said he could close her jaw manually if she would let him. After an hour-and-a-half of having it wide open, she was ready to try anything. He manually relieved whatever was stuck, and her mouth closed. She didn't open it very wide the rest of the weekend. I didn't even kiss her or anything. The unfortunate thing is Tennessee won 14-0.

I drove by the Mississippi State Museum of Progress today. It's still not open.

THE DAWGS ARE AN ITCH THAT DOESN'T GO AWAY WITH ONE SCRATCH

Darrell Huckaby

Huckaby, 56, is the author of Need Two *and* Need Four *and several other books. He is a UGA grad and does radio and speaking engagements. He teaches history at Heritage High School and lives in Conyers, Georgia.*

We were in Tuscaloosa, Alabama on a beautiful day for football. We were tailgating and sitting around enjoying the beautiful fall weather. We all commented on what a great day it was for football. Somebody said, "I can't think of another thing you can ask for." One of my friends said, "Well, I wish we had my piano." Someone asked, "What in the world would you want the piano for?" He answered, "Well.... That's where I left the damn tickets." He had come from home all the way to Tuscaloosa, Alabama...and had left the game tickets at home on top of the piano....

We were returning from the Cotton Bowl in Dallas, Texas, and decided to drop by New Orleans for a couple of days on the way home. On the way to New Orleans, the windshield wipers went out on our car, a '60 Camaro. We stopped at a little town in northern Louisiana and nobody could get a part to fix the car for at least several days. We didn't want to sit around that little town waiting for the part so we went to the hardware store ourselves and bought twine and tied the twine around the windshield wipers. It was about 38 degrees and there was sleet mixed in with the rain. We drove from northern Louisiana all the way to New Orleans, about three hours, with one guy pulling the windshield wipers one way and me pulling the windshield back the other way. We just operated the windshield wipers manually for a couple of hundred miles....

I have a really bad temper, and nothing is funny to me when Georgia is getting beat. It seems that wherever I go, fans from the other team manage to sit right beside me in the Georgia section. I've had a couple of instances where I've had problems with fans from the other team.

> ...'remember that time that 60-year-old man whipped your _ _ _ at the Georgia-Florida game.'"

A couple of years ago, we were leaving the Florida Gator Bowl—I know it's Alltel Stadium now but I still call it the Gator Bowl. We'd gotten beaten, as usual. I remember when we would beat them like a drum every year in Jacksonville during the pre-Spurrier days. We were going down a long ramp from the upper deck. We went around a curve in the ramp and four Florida students, in their early twenties, reached out and blocked my path and wouldn't let me by. I just smiled. I was determined to not have an incident. I stepped around to the left and they and their locked arms slid around also. I started around to the right, and they again locked arms and slid around to the right also. Finally, I looked at the biggest one of them and said, "Young man, I'm going to give you some real good advice. I'm going to try to walk around one more time. If I were you, I'd let me go. Otherwise you and your buddies here are going to be coming to this game for the next 50 years— every year—and every conversation you're going to have is going to begin with, 'remember that time that 60-year-old man whipped your _ _ _ at the Georgia-Florida game.'" He looked at me—I was only 53 at the time—but I guess he thought I looked pretty good for 60, so he just smiled at me and stepped aside to let me go through....

Back when there were only one or two games televised each week, the Georgia-Florida game wasn't on TV and it was tough to get a ticket for it. I had a friend, Becky Hutchins, who has since passed away. She was not able to go to the game because she had to go through dialysis treatment the day before the game. She had given her ticket to her brother, Jimmy. Well, Jimmy and I were in the parking lot at the Gator Bowl before the game, along with about 75-80,000 other people. Becky got up at four in the morning and drove to Jacksonville, after her dialysis treatment—leaving us without a ticket. She somehow found us in that parking lot in all that mass of humanity. We started into the game, and we were short one ticket so she said, "Don't worry, I'll take care of that." She told me to enter in front of her and her brother to go behind her. One of us walked in and handed in our ticket. Becky suddenly went into a dead faint, right onto the ground. The medical people rushed over, picked her up, and took her inside to the medical tent. She had a medical I-V placed in her arm. They gave her orange juice. She explained to them about having lupus and having just gone through the dialysis the day before. After five or 10 minutes, she said she was okay. They released her and the three of us just walked out of the medical tent right to the seats.

The BCS formula is actually a recipe for chili.

GOIN' TO THE DAWGS

I went to see Georgia play Arkansas in Fayetteville in 2000. Going into the game, Arkansas really thought they had a good chance to beat us. We beat them 38-7. When we walked out of that game there wasn't an Arkansas fan we passed that didn't thank us for coming and congratulate us on the win. You don't get that most places we go. I've got to give big kudos to those Arkansas fans. We went back a couple of years later and beat them again. They were annoyed but still gracious. They are real football fans.

I've been involved with the Annual Football Gala since '98. At the auction during David Pollack's senior year, he was holding a puppy that was a descendant of Uga's. You wouldn't believe the women that were all over David and Uga! We sold that puppy for $9,800 that night.

—SKIP BALCOMB, Athens, Georgia

During the 1980 Sugar Bowl trip, we went into Brennan's for brunch. My son, Tommy, was six-years old and very outgoing. He had all of his Georgia clothing on. A Notre Dame couple sat down next to us. Tommy said, "I'm for Georgia. Who are you'all for?" They said, "We're for Notre Dame." He said, "Yeah, I can tell." The Notre Dame guy said, "You really think Georgia has got a chance? This is going to be like boys playing men." Tommy said, "Oh, yeah, Georgia's definitely going win." The Notre Dame guy kept telling him, "Oh, you know Georgia hasn't got a chance. They haven't played anybody. They never played any big guys." Well, Georgia won the national championship. As we were walking out of the Super Dome, Tommy ran into the Notre Dame fans. He started yelling, "I told you Georgia was going to win." He walked right along beside them and gave them a hard time for about five minutes.

—TOM CLOUD, Georgia team student manager, '68-'69

Used to be the team would travel to games a day early because we would always have something planned to do. When we went to Houston in '67 we saw the NASA facility and the first space capsule that had gone into space. At the Cotton Bowl in '66, they had a big banquet for us at one of the nice hotels. We all sat down and looked at the table. There must have been 20 different pieces of flatware for each of us. Most of us were from Georgia. We'd never seen so much flatware. Everybody was watching somebody else to see which piece to use first. Most of us would use one fork and one knife for the whole meal.

—BRUCE YAWN, owner of Snooky's Restaurant, Statesboro, Georgia

For Christmas in '66, the church gave my wife and me a trip to the Cotton Bowl. That was the year Kent Lawrence returned a punt for a touchdown. We beat SMU when they had the receiver who became All-Pro. It was a great game. We flew down and had to land in Mississippi because of bad weather. We got to the stadium just in time for the kickoff. When we left there, the weather was still bad. We were in one of those 40-passenger Southern Airways planes that were flying then. We landed temporarily in Pine Bluff, Arkansas, and then flew on. Before we got to Athens, they said we were going to have to land in Atlanta or Chattanooga because we did not have radar in the Athens airport. I knew we did because my wife, who teaches science, had taken her class to the Athens airport to see the *weather* radar. I stopped the stewardess and said, "We do have radar there." My wife was trying to tell me that weather radar was not the same. The stewardess said, "No, honey, all you got in Athens is a big flashlight." We landed in Atlanta and drove home. We got in about two o'clock in the morning.

One time when we were playing LSU, they brought Mike the Tiger out on the field and rolled the cage down the sideline. When they got near our sideline Uga saw the cage and went bounding toward him. Mike, their tiger, backed into the other corner when he saw Uga. Our little group of about 10,000 people went bananas while their great massive tiger cowered before our yelping dog.

—CLAUDE MCBRIDE, Chaplain

My freshman year, 1978, the Georgia-Georgia Tech game was the most exciting game I've ever seen in person. My friends made a banner out of a bed sheet. If Auburn had beaten Alabama that same day, Georgia would win the SEC. The banner said, "Dawgs Love Sugar—Go Auburn." At halftime, a couple of us took it down to the track on the field. It was too tall for us to hold up. We grabbed a couple of kids who were sitting down there, and we put them on our shoulders. They held the banner up, and we marched it right in front of the Tech student section. All these Tech kids were coming down and were trying to walk through the banner or pull it out of our hands. There was one huge guy coming down where we were, with no shirt on, and I'm thinking, "Okay, now we're dead." He turned out to be a Georgia fan, and he started running interference for us, throwing the Tech kids into the hedges....

The 2001 Tennessee game was on TV and I was watching it. That was the one that we came back to win it with seconds left on the clock. We had a split-level house and I was watching the game downstairs. My daughter was only eight at the time, so my wife had her up in the playroom watching the game 'cause I tend to get a little animated sometimes. She took her upstairs to shield her ears from my "colorful exuberance" so I was downstairs and they were upstairs. I had already, after an earlier play, thought the officials had missed a call, and went running upstairs to see if my wife had seen it. I slipped on the stairs and broke my pinky finger. Then, Georgia comes back down the field and wins the game. I jumped up out of my chair, was literally jumping up and down, just in absolute joy at winning—it was the first time we had won at Tennessee in a long time. I ended up tearing my patella tendon. I was lying on the floor, hollering for help. They were upstairs cheering...they just thought that I was cheering, and it took a while for them to realize I was hurt....

In 1994, a friend of mine got Georgia-South Carolina tickets from a client who was a big South Carolina booster. They were really good seats, but we were right in the middle of all these Gamecocks. My buddy kept telling us, "You can't get too animated." That was the year Hines Ward started at tailback as a freshman. We won the game 24-21. Hines had a huge game, and you could see he was going to be something special. Needless to say, we did get a little animated and the 'little old ladies' around us were not very pleased. The South Carolina fans are great people. Their team has not done anything in football in their entire history yet, every year, they think they're going to win the SEC...and they pack that stadium! Their stadium is almost as big as ours. Coming off a 1-10 season, they'll still sell out. Everybody says they're great fans. We've never had any kind of an incident tailgating up there. They're always good to talk to, but it's just so funny to see that they really think they're on the same level with us. ...but, they're not!

—JAMIE CLARK, 47, Athens

I was visiting Beijing, China, with my wife Cristal and Harold Linnenkohl and his wife Linda back in 2006. There are over 1.3 billion people in China and Beijing has a population of over twelve and a half million people. One day we were walking through the crowded streets and came upon three young Chinese men all wearing UGA baseball caps. I was really surprised that among all the people that we encountered in China, we probably bumped into the only Georgia Bulldog fans in the country. We were really amazed. When we returned to Georgia I learned that the Georgia Redcoat band had recently visited China and had given hats to some Chinese as souvenirs when they were there.

—STEVE STANCIL, Canton, Georgia

There's nothing on earth like game day in Athens. I wish I could take all the people here in Florida who aren't Dawg fans. One Saturday in Athens would probably convert them.

Living in Bradenton, Florida, I'm definitely in a hostile environment. Especially with us losing as many games to Florida as we've lost to them lately. It's amazing to me how many Dawg fans I do see down here. I look for them everywhere. When I see Florida plates with UGA stickers or a "G" sticker on the back, I always honk.

I was in an Albertson's parking lot in Parish, Florida about three months before we started house hunting. I had dropped my fiancée off to go inside the grocery store and pulled into a parking spot to wait for her. I saw a Ford Explorer with a "G" sticker on the back. Inside sat a man, a woman and two children. I rolled down my window and asked him if he was a Dawg fan, and he said, "Hell, yeah." We struck up a conversation about Georgia for 10 or 15 minutes, until his wife leaned over and laid on the horn. They left soon after that. I enjoyed talking with the guy so much I gave him my business card. I said, "Listen, I know you're down here in enemy territory like I am, so if you need somebody to watch the ball game with, give me a call.

Recently my fiancée and I have been looking for a house. I just got pre-approved for my first home loan. The last neighborhood we drove into one very long day is called Chelsea Oaks. We rode around and found a house we liked. We got out and walked around the house taking pictures. As we got back into the car, I looked at the neighbor's house. In the driveway sat the same navy blue Explorer with a "G" on the back that I had seen three months before. The same guy was out doing some yard work. I went over and talked to him again. "Man, I think this is fate." We will probably buy that house.

—JACK WAYBRIGHT, Athens-born, now living in Bradenton, Florida

The last time LSU played at Georgia, they had their cars, fans, buses with sound systems on top pulled into every conceivable spot on the University campus, playing every kind of music you can imagine, including zydeco. Many of the fans were well into their cups by seven-thirty in the morning when my wife and I walked across campus as we do before home games just to look at the crowd. By noon they were really flying high and screaming a cheer I had never hear before. "Hot boudin, cold couscous, come on team, let's poosh, poosh, poosh." Boudin is a sausage. The LSU people are so kind to their friends and opponents alike. They'll pull you into their tent, pavilion, van—whatever they've got going—and offer you food and drink. They're amazing people with their outgoing nature, but they are rowdy....

> One of Dawgs leans over, as this alligator goes by, and goes chomp! He bit the nose off the Gator!

I was sitting in the Gator Bowl back in the seventies. Florida traditionally gets the most seats together so they have critical mass on us. There are small parts of the stadium with mixed fans—Florida Gator colors and Georgia Bulldog colors both show. Most of the time, the rivalry was fairly good-natured. I was sitting by one of the walkways with my wife and another couple. Just in front of us were two guys in red and black. As we were sitting there, up through the passageway came three guys—they must have been bakers—carrying a huge alligator made out of bread! They held it above their heads to keep other people from grabbing it, not realizing they are walking it at eye level of these two old Bulldogs sitting in front of us. One of Dawgs leans over, as this alligator goes by, and goes chomp! He bit the nose off the Gator! It was easily one of the funniest things I've seen at a ball game.

—LEN DAVIS, 64, Athens, GA

My husband Gil had gotten a stipend, a little scholarship, to go to the University in Erlangen, just outside of Nuremberg, Germany. It's a sister university to UGA. He went over in September 1980, and I joined him in December. The '81 Sugar Bowl game was New Year's Day, but we had no way to watch it. We sat in the international dormitory and listened to it on Armed Forces Radio. About a month later, we were at the Hofbrauhaus in Munich having one of those huge steins of beer. We looked across a couple of tables and saw some kids with Notre Dame tee shirts on. Gil was very good in his language skills. He had an excellent accent, and he blended right in. He walked over, very friendly, speaking in German, "Oh, how are you? I see you're from Notre Dame." About all they understood was Notre Dame. They were bobbing their heads and pointing to their tee shirts. He continued the conversation in German for a few moments, then switched into perfect Southern and said, "How about them Dawgs?" Their faces just fell. It was a priceless moment.

—CHERYL CHANDLER, UGA '82, president, Central California UGA Alumni Association

Because I'm a high school band director, for years I would leave Gainesville for the Georgia-Florida game in Jacksonville at midnight or one on Saturday morning. One night we'd gone about 20 miles. The police stopped us in Jefferson, Georgia, for drinking. He looked in and the car, but all I had was a cup of coffee. I told him where I was going. He said, "Well, you looked  like you were swerving a little bit." He let us go. We got to Jacksonville about eight o'clock in the morning. I got out and walked around to the back of the van, and it became obvious why he stopped us. In the back window were two cases of Killians Irish Red.

One year, my high school football game was on a Saturday night, the same Saturday night as the afternoon Georgia-Florida game. I had a friend from Jasper, Georgia, who had a pilot's license and a plane. He picked up my principal and me at six o'clock the morning of the game. We flew down, watched the game until the early part of the fourth quarter then flew back to Gainesville. As we landed I saw my band buses going by. We got in the car and caught up with the buses so I was there for my football game.

I love going up to Rocky Flop...excuse me, Rocky Top. I have my own verses to the song. One year we were tailgating in a huge parking lot where there were some Georgia fans who had a tent and had a speaker system. My friend encouraged me to go up and sing my song. There were maybe a thousand people in that parking lot, and everybody got quiet as I sang my "Rocky Flop" song. I enjoyed that, and, we won that day too.

Here's how my "Rocky Flop" goes:

> Once I had a test on Rocky Flop
> Question on the test was "spell cat"
> Told my teacher that wouldn't help me
> In my job at the laundree-mat
> When my football days are over
> I gotta get a job its true
> With my bach-el-ors degree
> I can deliver pizzas to you

> Once I had a date on Rocky Flop
> Homecoming Queen to be
> On the date that moonlit night
> She barked a raccoon up a tree

> (Chorus)

> Rocky Flop will always be
> Handing out free degrees
> Good ole Rocky Flop
> Just don't tell the SEC

The best fans you ever see are at Mississippi, tailgating at The Grove. Tents are set up with lights all around and elaborate spreads with candelabras on the tables. And they invite everybody who walks by to join them. At night after the game, they put the spread back out again, and they're there forever. It's really quite an event. They're the best fans I've ever been around, other than my Dawg fans.

I'll tell you how much of a fanatic I am; I have a Bobcat scanner. I take it to the away games. All I've got to do is set it to the frequency from the press box to the production truck, and I get all the Munson calls, and I don't get the commercials. I get to hear everything they talk about in between. That's really fun. All you've got to do is go to Wal-Mart and buy a Bobcat scanner. They're about $39.00.

> ...set it to the frequency from the press box to the production truck, and I get all the Munson calls, and I don't get the commercials.

—MERCER CROOK, band director, UGA grad

I have a fully restored 1928 Model-A truck, painted red and black with the Bulldog painted on the radiator. It's covered, and I've hauled Uga in it a couple of times in the homecoming parade. We also hauled him when we had to get a grill inside Sonny Seiler's tailgate and in the St. Patrick's Day parade in Savannah. They started having homecoming parades six or seven years ago, and the parade committee knew I had this truck. They called me about it, and, of course, I was honored. We've hauled the cheer-leaders and Athletic Director Damon Evans and his family and other folks. We take it to some tailgates. At homecoming, we usually carry it over and tailgate with it. When we built the car, Sonny Seiler was very impressed with what we had done. The name of the car is Uga's Ride.

We always go to the Georgia-Florida game. We take our motor home with a bunch of friends immediately after the game the previous week. We usually stay near the stadium in one of the parking lots. We're in the Bulldog Motor Coach Club, which has about 100 members. We'll caravan to a lot of the away games. We always take a big grill, and we all have a big cookout for about 120 people and a lot of good fellowship.

> I'm not one to fight, but I hit him right in his privates and doubled him over.

During the 1980 national championship game I was sitting in the stands and we were about to get beat. There were Florida fans behind me. One of them had been giving us a good bit of grief. When we finally went ahead, I turned around to him and said, "How about them Bulldogs?" He got really mad and took a punch at me. I'm not one to fight, but I hit him right in his privates and doubled him over. He rolled down the stands, and I thought I was going to have to fight the rest of his buddies. They said, "Sir, we apologize. We're so glad you took care of him. We won't have to deal with him no more."

I enjoy going out to Arkansas. Those are some of the greatest fans to be around. They've got a real parking lot for RVs with hookups and everything. We don't have anything like that.

Kentucky is a great place to go because of the horse racing. They've changed the horse racing schedules on us, but, used to be we'd get up there the last week of horse racing and go to the races. Those fans up there are classy. They dress to go to a football game like we dress to go to a formal dinner and do the same at the races too. One time, I hit a trifecta on a long shot and won about $2,000. That's my greatest memory. Now that they've changed the dates, we have to drive over to Louisville to Churchill Downs to see the races.

—FRANK SAXON, 71, Canton, Georgia

Georgia football is the number one priority of my family in the fall. It's what we do every Saturday. Nobody dares make plans to do anything else on game weekends. We wouldn't even die before a Georgia weekend because we'd have to put the funeral off until Monday or Tuesday. One of my twin sons lives up near Washington D.C. now, but he tries to make it home for at one or two ball games a year. It's something that keeps us all together, something we all enjoy, my dad, myself, my boys.

The best trip we took as a family was to the Outback Bowl in Tampa when Georgia played **WISCONSIN*** about 10 years ago. That was about the time the boys were getting ready to go off to college. It was one of the last trips we all took as a family. The weather was great, and we did a lot of family things, and we won the ball game.

We have a place in Daytona, so we stay there when we go to the Georgia-Florida game. We make a week out of it. Twenty years ago, my wife and I took my brother-in-law and sister-in-law to the game. The weather turned bad at halftime and it started raining, so they went to a bar across the street. I don't believe in leaving a ball game before it's over, so we stayed. After the game was over—Florida won, unfortunately—we were going back to the car. My sister-in-law, Vicki, had a little too much to drink in the bar. Some Florida fans were giving her some lip. She's a real petite little thing. She turned around and said, "If you'll get your ugly—over here, I'll just whip it." I was the only one in the group who was of any size, and I knew who was going to have to fight them. I put my hand over her mouth and rushed her to the car. We tease her about that a lot.

—STEVE STANCIL, UGA '75

I thought the Kentucky fans and the Vanderbilt fans were very gracious. They never had very good teams, but even when they beat us a couple of years ago, they were gracious winners. Everybody I encountered on the street after the game was so excited about their team winning, and they congratulated us on a good game. I didn't hear one disparaging word.

The worst fans, no doubt, are Gators. We've been to Jacksonville three or four years now. We usually go down on Thursday. It's all Georgia fans Thursday and Friday. Then on Saturday, it's like they crawl out from under a rock.

—JAY ABBOTT, father of Bulldog player Chris Abbott '03-'06

The '96 Auburn game was at Auburn, and some friends and I were planning to go over there. We tried to get tickets through the

*Arnold Schwarzenegger graduated from the University of WISCONSIN in 1979.

Georgia ticket office and they were sold out. We tried to get tickets through the Auburn ticket office and they were sold out. We were originally planning to get in the car, ride over there, understanding that we would have to pay a scalper some exorbitant price to get in to go to the game. But, everybody had something come up. One guy had to work. One guy didn't feel like he had enough money to pay for the ticket. Another guy had family coming into town so we decided not to go. That wound up being the quadruple overtime, historic Georgia victory—probably the most exciting game we'd ever played against our oldest rival. I still stay in touch with those guys...and still give them a hard time, to this day, that because they had to go visit their family and go to work.... I told them they should have quit their job, bit the bullet, spend a little bit of money, tell your grandma you'll see her the next time...and go to the dang game.

—T. KYLE KING. 38, '90 UGA grad

> We bought every flashlight this little store had, duct taped them all on the hood and off we went.

One year we drove to the Alabama game in my motor home. We drove past a breakdown on the side of the road and it was Coach Dicky Clark who was driving to the game on Saturday morning. We picked him up and took him straight to the Alabama game in the motor home. We were partying real hard, and, of course, Coach Clark could not party at all, but, he did have to get to the game too.

Another year, I had a brand new Lincoln Continental with less than 1,000 miles on it. We're driving down through the back roads because the Interstates weren't through there yet. Right when the car hit 1,000 miles, the lights cut off. It was very dark. We pull into the next town which had a little station but nobody there knew how to fix our problem. We were going to have to go on down another road about 40 miles to LaGrange. We bought every flashlight this little store had, duct taped them all on the hood and off we went. We got to LaGrange where there was one truck stop. They straight-wired the battery to the lights...every time we stopped, we had to take the battery off—but, we made it.

I was going to Kentucky to a game. Three other guys couldn't leave when I did, but were going to join me there and stay with me in my motor home. I broke down in London, Kentucky—the motor home caught fire and burned right to the ground. At 2:30 in the morning, I was standing out there, and the fire department was just pulling in...and the guys who were planning to stay with me drove by. They had caught up with me, I got in with them, we went to the game, got motel rooms and came back after the game.

—CRAIG HERTWIG, UGA player '72-'74

In '96, we went to the South Carolina game in Columbia. I went with three college buddies, Travis Rice, Jeff Rogers, Bryan Pritchett and Jayson Akridge. We were going to tailgate and grill out. Unfortunately there were four of us in the car and no room for a grill. Travis got one of those big metal turkey pans and took the cooking grids out of his grill. What he was going to do was put the charcoal down in the big turkey pan and the grill across the top and cook the chicken on top of that. He didn't want to put the pan directly down on the ground because it would get so hot. He had gotten one of those heavy plastic crates. He was thinking that it was good, solid, sturdy plastic so it would hold up. He puts the plastic crate down...puts the metal turkey pan on top of it...puts the charcoal in it, lights the charcoal, puts the grill on top and puts the chicken on the grill. It starts, as we should have figured, melting that crate because of the heat. The pan starts sinking down into this melting plastic crate which was okay at first...but, then it started to tip. It was hotter in one part than another so it tipped more on one side. It's gradually tilting to where eventually the flame catches the crate on fire. There's this horrible smell coming up from it. We didn't have anything like oven mitts so we grabbed a newspaper and grabbed the metal grill to pick it up to keep the chicken from being ruined. We had to do something—so we kicked the crate over, knocking the charcoal out of it so we could pour some water on the crate and put the fire out. Now, we've got half-cooked chicken and hot plastic and charcoal there on the ground. The guys around us—probably most of them had been drinking—and they were really enjoying the show. Somebody gets the idea—he's got a couple of empty beer cans. They grab empty beer cans from everyone and set up a ring of these empties around the pile of smoldering charcoal on the ground. We were able to put the grill up on top of the empty beer cans over the charcoal and finished cooking the chicken and actually had some tasty chicken to eat before the game.

—T. KYLE KING, UGA Law '97, Hampton, GA

There was this one game at Georgia Tech, as crazy as that is, it might have been '90, and Georgia was supposed to lose to Georgia Tech. They were just a powerhouse then. We ended up scoring a last-second touchdown in the corner where seven of us were sitting so we were able to see the whole thing develop. It was one of those moments where—it was all of 30 seconds—it felt like a lifetime. We were watching this guy get away from the cornerbacks and catch the ball in the end zone, literally 20 yards in front of us. You could see the deflation of the six Georgia Tech buddies right there...as dog bones were being thrown at me at that point in time. That was the best Georgia Tech experience ever for me.

—GREG ERBS, 39, lives in Cummings GA

About 15 years ago, my mother and father were going to a Georgia-Florida game. My mother had rheumatoid arthritis very bad. They were walking toward the stadium and had to cross over a small ditch. My mother couldn't make it across. My father was elderly and not able to help her get across by himself. A Georgia fan, also on his way to the game, stopped and helped them. My mom and dad are Florida fans and were in their orange and blue, and the Georgia fan was in the red and black. Daddy got on one side, and the Georgia guy got on the other side. Between the two of them, they were able to help mom across the ditch. My mom and dad thanked the Georgia fan for his gallantry. At that time, another fan, who was also going to the game, said, "I would never help a Gator." The gentleman from Georgia who had helped them cocked an eye at him and said, "Mister, I'll help a lady any day." My mom was glad to have run into a Southern gentleman on that day.

I've never sat down and watch the Georgia-Florida game with my family. They still live in Florida, and I live out here in California. The way it works out, whichever team loses, that fan calls the other to congratulate them on the win. Georgia football has probably been the one experience that keeps me connected to the University, and to my time there.

—CARL GUILFORD, 51, Bakersfield, California

When you're young, your parents tell you not to talk to strangers. Well, I didn't really listen to that. I like to talk to people. Some friends and I were at Ole Miss for the game, and our quarterback was not doing very well. He'd already thrown two interceptions. A couple of rowdy Ole Miss fans were seated across the aisle from us. I got up to get something to eat and leaned over to make a joke to the Ole Miss guys. "I'll tell you what you guys can

> These Ole Miss boys are being drunk and obnoxious, and these Georgia boys haven't done anything wrong."

do to win this game, make sure our quarterback keeps throwing it like he's doing." All I got out of my mouth was, "I'll tell you what you can do...." Three of the Ole Miss guys stood up. One of them threw a fist at me and said, "I'll tell you what you can do, you Georgia SOB..." I said, "Whoa! Okay! Time out!" I know when to walk away from it. But, my friend, who is about 6'3", is an old Mississippi boy. He was a physical education doctoral student at UGA at the time and had a little too much bourbon. He saw that his buddy needed some backup. He rallied to my defense. He said, "What's the problem here?" The Ole Miss guys said, "Oh, you're the problem!" By this time, people were getting pushed. We were making a scene.

The cops came up and were about to throw us out of the stadium, when out of nowhere, this little 95-year-old angel decked out in Ole Miss red and blue, came down out of the stands. She tapped the policeman on the shoulder, and said, "Officer, I saw the whole thing. These Ole Miss boys are drunk and obnoxious, and these Georgia boys haven't done anything wrong." The cop said, "Good enough for me." The Ole Miss guys were told if they bothered anybody, Georgia or Ole Miss, the rest of the game, the cops wouldn't think twice about throwing them out. That little sweet lady was the only reason that me and my friends got to see the end of the game. I was not expecting that. You see somebody coming down, wearing the Ole Miss colors, you think, "Oh God. Here we go. Here's a witness who didn't see anything, but just because I'm wearing tons of red and black, it's not going to be in my favor." Football in the South is almost a religion. You don't question someone else's religious fervor! I was very, very thankful and scratching my head thinking, "Oh man, this shouldn't have happened. This is an anomaly."

—MATTHEW FOSTER, diehard Bulldog fan

When Clint Eastwood directed the movie, "Midnight in the Garden of Good and Evil," in Savannah, he told Mrs. Cecelia Seiler that he was going to make her dog a national celebrity. She corrected him. "Mr. Eastwood, Uga is already a national celebrity. You don't have to make him into one."...

I went to a game at Mississippi State when Herschel was playing. Those folks out there were as nice to us as they could be. Out in the tailgate area prior to the game they were bringing us food and desserts. They just insisted we accept the food. We only had boxes of KFC, so the food the ladies brought us was well accepted. They posed for pictures with everybody. They were very friendly. That's the best experience I've ever had—Mississippi State. We were treated like you should be treated if you're a visitor in somebody's home. They welcomed us.

—ROBERT WESTMORELAND, '71, Ellijay, Ga.

...someone in the car was saying that message boards were nothing but trash.

I probably know fifty or so posters from the internet, in fact, I go to UGA road games almost exclusively with guys I know from the internet. I was driving to the Alabama game this year and someone in the car was saying that message boards were nothing but trash. I reminded him that if it weren't for the internet we wouldn't even be in the car together. We had all met on the *Dawg Run* or the *Dawg Vent* and then through email. When I walk into a game, usually two or three people will call out my internet handle. My internet handle is ButtsMehre, after the athletic heritage building at UGA that was named after Wally Butts and Harry Mehre. I always thought that it was a funny name, so I use it. It's a strange name for a building but think of the alternative...the MehreButts building?

Tech fans are bad; Just ask Dog44. He hates Tech and has just one thing to say about Tech fans that sums it all up, "Tech lies and cheats!" That says it all. They used to fly a banner over the Georgia-Georgia Tech game that read "Tech Lies and Cheats!" They don't do it any more because they have banned aircraft from flying over stadiums. When everybody purchased a brick at Gate 6 and had their brick placed there with their name on it as the donor, well, Dog44 purchased one and placed it there and it said, you guessed it, "Tech Lies and Cheats!" I've said before that SEC fans are all great...well they are southern and that's why. Tech fans are not from the South.

> They used to fly a banner over the Georgia-Georgia Tech game that read "Tech Lies and Cheats!"

People from Georgia, after Tech fans attacked the Maryland band, after they threw bottles at Bear Bryant, after they threw fish at the Notre Dame team, people ask "What's with people from Georgia?" We have to tell them that Tech fans are not from the South. They are eighty percent or so from New Jersey, New York and other places north of here. Bear Bryant wouldn't even allow his players to eat food from Georgia because he didn't want to leave a dime from Alabama here...all because of Tech! Years ago, Tech used to hose down Grant Field to slow down fast backs from visiting teams. They once blamed Notre Dame for doing that to them...just further proof that Tech lies and cheats...they blamed others for doing what, really, they used to do!

Unbelievably, Tech also has had an absolute stranglehold of SEC officiating for my whole life. For the last 25 years Bobby Gaston, a Tech letterman, has been the head of SEC referees and often attended the Georgia-Georgia Tech games at Grant Field. His presence was well-known to the SEC refs doing the games and they knew how they were expected to call the games. He was also instrumental in banning Mark Richt's no-huddle offense back in 2006. "I did it so Mark Richt wouldn't eat everybody's lunch", Gaston said when asked about the rule change. Thank God he finally announced his retirement. But, then he announced his replacement...another Tech man. Clearly, **Tech lies and cheats!**

—*JOE SUGGS*, artist, North Springs, GA

 In 1965 during Vince Dooley's second year Georgia opened the season against defending champion Alabama and we beat them. A few weeks later Georgia flew up to Ann Arbor to play Michigan. Georgia was a big underdog, Michigan was the defending Rose Bowl Champion and they were huge. Georgia was fast but small. We ended up beating Michigan 15-7 and the whole town of Athens just went bonkers. Probably about ten or fifteen thousand people showed up at our little airport to meet the team returning from the victory. The plane landed and the crowd started chanting "Damn good team! Damn good team!" The plane taxied over to where the crowd was while they continued chanting "Damn good team, damn good team!" Well, when they finally opened the door, this little old lady was the first one out and she looked around at the crowd, somewhat confused, and the crowd fell silent. Suddenly some smart _ _ _ in the crowd started to yell, "Wrong damn plane, wrong damn plane!" The crowd picked up the chant and kept on chanting until the real plane carrying the Georgia team finally pulled up to the crowd....

During the 2001 season, I got three tickets to the Georgia-Ole Miss game in Oxford, Mississippi. I asked two friends if they wanted to go and they said yes. One friend said he wouldn't be able to leave until 8 p.m. Friday because of his job. Well, on Friday he calls late in the afternoon and says he can't go at all. So I called the other friend and by 6 p.m. Friday evening we are on the road. I told him that Interstate 20 goes directly across Alabama and Mississippi and then we turn right to get to Oxford. I didn't realize that Interstate 20 turns south at Birmingham and by the time I realized my mistake we were way south of where we wanted to go. We turned north and instead of a six-hour or so drive, we ended up getting to Oxford around 6 a.m. It was cold that night and we struggled through the night just to keep awake! We wanted to get a motel room and get a few hours sleep but couldn't. We had to drive back to Tupelo just to get a room. We did get a room, slept for about two to three hours, woke up and drove to Oxford, went to the game and after the game we drove back to Georgia. Quite an effort just to go to an away game...and all because I just didn't take the time to look at a map!

—AARON JONES, 26, Tyrone, GA

I was at the Tech game in 2001 and we were coming off a three-game losing streak to them which came off a seven-game losing streak to us. Three loses in a row to Tech is pretty much unbearable to us and I'm out there at Grant Field sitting about fifty rows up in the stadium and I see some guy walking along the concourse at field level and he's holding up three fingers. I held up seven fingers representing our longest winning streak against Tech. Somehow, he notices me and holds up eight fingers representing the longest winning streak by either team which Tech had against us in the late forties through the early fifties, which left me with only one option so I held up one finger and I'm sure you can guess which one it was!

—DICK FOX, Marietta, GA

Name the
'Ole Miss Coach...
Win Valuable Prizes!

I ran into a Florida
fan yesterday. Then,
I backed up and ran
into him again.

Chapter 8

Fandemonium

Open the Gates and Open Them Wide,
Dawg Fans are Coming Inside!!!

THE NCAA—
A WHOLLY-OWNED SUBSIDIARY OF NIKE

Sam Hendrix

Hendrix is retired and lives in Signal Mountain, Tennessee, just outside Chattanooga. He went to Georgia Southern when they didn't have a football team so he adopted the Bulldogs.

The Boise State game a few years ago was getting a lot of hype in the media about the potential upset of Georgia in what would be the biggest game in Boise State history. They had never played in front of 93,000 fans. One of the stories that ran was about Dan Miller, a Boise police officer who was serving in Iraq training Iraqi policemen. He was going to fly in to see his son, an offensive lineman, play in this big game. The flight was 12-14 hours long and was going to cost thousands of dollars. I read that story and thought what a great moment to share with your son, not to mention what a great service he's providing for his country in Baghdad. It occurred to me that as Americans there must be something we could do to help him pay his way here to enjoy his son's biggest game. I posted a comment about it, and instantly people began responding on-line. What we had to do was get it organized, they said. We had to find out how much money we needed, how to handle the money, and what businesses we might get to join us. We needed to help Mr. Miller for what he had done for us and also to allow him to enjoy an experience that, as fathers, we would all want to have with our sons.

I left to play **GOLF***, and when I got back the idea had really blown up. Somebody had suggested it might be an NCAA violation if we paid expenses for parents to attend a game. That didn't

---

*While playing **GOLF** in 1567, Mary Queen of Scots was informed that her husband, Lord Darnley, had been murdered. She finished the round.

---

make sense to me because it wasn't one of our players we were covering. Sure enough, someone checked with the NCAA and found that this would indeed violate their rules. We had to let it die down, although people were outraged about it.

Afterward I got calls for interviews. I told the people on ESPN, "It's pretty hard to confuse me with a Boise State fan. We're not trying to recruit his son. He already has a position at Boise State and loves his school, so it defies common sense."

I said, "I really think the NCAA is losing perspective on what's in compliance and what constitutes a problem in this country. People are really endorsing this idea." ESPN's Cold Pizza did an interview with me about the NCCA compliance rules. I told them, "I'm a huge Georgia fan, but I'm also a big college football fan, and this was going to be a great moment for Boise State and Georgia fans."

> ... the NCAA is losing perspective on what's in compliance and what constitutes a problem in this country.

Sports talk stations around the country picked it up, and I did interviews with them. Yahoo! did a story on it. It got a lot of good publicity for Georgia and bad publicity for the NCAA. The Georgia fans were very supportive of it, but, unfortunately, it did not come to pass. Mr. Miller came to the game, but I never got a chance to meet him.

HE'S NOT GOING BALD.
HE'S JUST GETTING MORE HEAD

Michael Woods

Woods, 57, Colbert, Georgia, grew up in Athens and is known to Bulldog fans all around the world. He's not hard to spot. He is the guy at the game with the Georgia Bulldog painted on his head! He recently won the Aaron's Southern Sports Award as the "Super Fan of the Year" for the SEC.

My dad started the whole "Big Dawg" persona during the 1980 season. He used to drive the team bus for Erk Russell and the defense. The team talked my dad into shaving his head and painting a Bulldog up there. The first time he did it was at the 1981 Sugar Bowl. He shaved his head, and an art student painted a Bulldog on it. We went to the game and watched Georgia beat **NOTRE DAME*** for the national championship. Daddy went to every home and away game up until he passed away in '87. After that, I sat in my daddy's seats, and everybody kept saying, "Mike, you've got to keep it going. You've got to keep it going." My wife started painting my head in '91 and has been doing it ever since. We call it a family tradition now. My younger son is going to continue after I pass away. He just said, "Daddy, I hope you live a long time." He wasn't in any hurry to shave his head.

Daddy worked at Sanford Stadium, and my brother and I would go with him to the stadium on game days. I started at six years old, selling peanuts at the stadium. That way, my brother and I

When Knute **ROCKNE and seven others were killed in a 1931 plane crash, it was the largest disaster in U.S. aviation history up until that time.*

would get in to watch Georgia play. We were told, "Boys, when you sell out of peanuts, you get to sit down and watch the rest of the game." We always sold all of our peanuts by halftime. I went from selling peanuts to selling Coca-Cola to parking cars to buying tickets. I've missed one game in the 37 years I've been buying tickets. I had back surgery and wasn't able to go. I would have gone then, if they would have let me out of the hospital.

> My dad started the whole "Big Dawg" persona during the 1980 season.

The first time I went to Sanford Stadium, it was unreal. It was the best place I'd ever been. I loved the atmosphere. There were so many people. I enjoyed watching the football team doing the best they could do. It was so much fun pulling and cheering for them and just enjoying the day! There's nothing better than being in Sanford Stadium on game day—nothing. When I'm in the stands or in the end zone when the players come on the field, I do everything I can to keep them pumped up.

The LSU road trip in 2001 was one of the best I've been on. I had the Bulldog on my head, and the LSU fans treated us like I was one of them. Heck, they fed us the entire time, and it wasn't like we didn't have our own food. We never got to cook one drop of the stuff we took. They fed us the whole time we were there. When we left, they made us take all kinds of Cajun food home with us. It was great. My younger son went with us. About ten o'clock on Friday night, they brought a pizza over for him. That is tailgating! You meet a bunch of friends like that, and you're from out of town, and they make you feel at home.

I got to meet Herschel Walker personally. Not only is he a great football player, he's one of the nicest people I've ever met in my life. He's got not only a football story, but he's got a great personal story that will absolutely break you down if you listen to him. I raise English bulldogs. Herschel got a solid white bulldog from me. He bought it for himself, and he took it to his mother for her to watch while he was moving to Texas. His mama wouldn't give it back to him. She kept it.

I don't listen to the games on the radio when I'm at a game. Don't get me wrong, I love Mr. Munson. I love listening to him, but I'm not able to do it. I'm doing everything I can to keep the players playing hard. I love his excitement. When he gets excited, you can't help but get excited. You might not even be pulling for Georgia, but when he gets excited, you get excited, too.

I've met Mr. Munson several times. He's one of the nicest guys I've ever met. I don't know who's going to take his place when he decides to retire. It's going to be hard for somebody to take his place.

Can you read this?
Miami Hurricanes can't.

JIMMY MATTHEWS OUTKICKED HIS COVERAGE WHEN HE MARRIED THIS GAL

Dee Matthews

Matthews, 58, serves on the boards of many civic and other organizations such as the Boys and Girls Clubs of Albany, the Friends of Phoebe Putney Hospital, and was 1999 UGA Alumnus of the Year. She is the former Chairman of the Georgia Sports Hall of Fame and lives in Albany, Georgia with her legendary husband, Jimmy.

We were on our way to Jacksonville for the Georgia-Florida game with our friend, Lewis Grizzard, who was a well-known columnist and humorist who passed away in 1994. He was Georgia graduate and a huge Bulldog fan, who traveled to games with us often. The weather that day was not expected to be good. As we discussed the cold he mentioned that he might not be prepared for nasty weather and suggested we stop so he could get a few things. We stopped and ended up buying almost an entire outfit for him. Thank God he didn't write a column about it...something he often did! I can't remember who won the game, but I can tell you this: Lewis was prepared!...

Years ago, we traveled to Nashville for the Vanderbilt game. We had heard a lot about the new Astroturf everyone was getting and Vanderbilt had just installed their **ASTROTURF***. So, we were anxious to see it. My husband, Jimmy, and I and another couple went to the stadium and noticed that the gates to the field were open. We walked in and saw Sonny Seiler and Uga.

*An announcer once asked Tug McGraw about the difference between **ASTROTURF** and grass. Tug replied, "I don't know. I have never smoked Astroturf."

The Vanderbilt athletic director was showing Sonny and some other folks around. He was so proud of their new Astroturf. Sonny saw me and said, "Dee, why don't you walk Uga." I took the leash, and we walked around. Well, the dog decided he needed to relieve his social pressures. He proceeded to do just that, right on top of Vanderbilt's brand new Astroturf! The athletic director had a fit, "Who's gonna clean this up? Who's gonna clean this up?" I handed the leash back to Sonny and said, "It's his dog."...

Several years ago at the Georgia-Florida game, we were in a Georgia parking lot—they sell tickets just to Georgia people so we can have a parking lot of our own. A husband and wife were tailgating close to us. We were partying and having a time. She was a Bulldog fan, and he was a Florida fan. Just before the game she and the rest of us were carrying on about how we were gonna beat the Gators, and he said "If Georgia wins the game you can kiss my a _ _!" Well, Georgia won. After the game we were celebrating at the tailgate and someone said to him, "What about your pregame promise?" With everyone in the crowd egging him on, he pulled his pants down a little bit and she kissed...to the great delight of many, many Bulldog fans. That's one of the funniest sights we ever saw in Jacksonville!...

When Larry Munson lived in Atlanta, he would stay at the Holiday Inn Express in Athens, where we always stay. One morning we were having breakfast and talking about the new suites they had just built in Sanford Stadium. I mentioned that I had not seen them. Larry said, "Walk to the stadium with me. I'll take you up to the press box, and you can see those new suites for yourself." We got up to one of the suites. I proceeded to take hold of the doorknob. When I tried to open it all the burglar alarms in Sanford Stadium went off. Munson said, "I don't know who did that." I said, "I don't either. Lets get the hell out of here!"...

We watched Ray Goff grow up. He is from South Georgia, and we watched him mature into a college star. He's got a warm, loving personality and never meets a stranger. When Lewis Grizzard was in the hospital at Emory—he was particularly ill during spring football practice—Ray would get in his car after practice in Athens and drive to Atlanta and sit by Lewis' bedside and tell him all about practice. Ray would stay with Lewis until he feel asleep. Then Ray would drive back to Athens late at night.

After Ray completed his football playing days at Georgia, he signed with a professional football team. They gave him a signing bonus. When he didn't make the team, he returned the signing bonus. We asked "What are you doing?" He said, "Well, I didn't make the team, and I don't deserve the money, so I'm not going to accept it." That's the kind of guy he is.

Lewis Grizzard had asked in his will if...at least part of his ashes could be sprinkled...at Sanford Stadium.

Lewis Grizzard had asked in his will if, when he died, at least part of his ashes could be sprinkled on the field at Sanford Stadium. We got special permission as close friends and family from Coach Dooley, who was then athletic director, and he agreed to let us spread some of Lewis' ashes at midfield in Sanford Stadium. We did.

THESE 7 THINGS ARE THE 10 REASONS HE'S A BULLDOG FAN

Harry Cashin

Cashin has been practicing law in Atlanta for 47 years. He is 75 and a major college football fan and historian. He has four children and ten grandchildren. Cashin was a close friend of one of the great Bulldog fans, the late Tom Watson Brown. Friends still wonder how two lawyers like them could get in so much trouble through all those years and survive!

I was in school with that great, great Georgia supporter and owner of the Georgia Bulldog, Sonny Seiler. We were in numerous organizations together, including the inter-fraternity council. He was a Sigma Chi. I was a Pi K A. I was in the service in 1956, when he produced the first Bulldog, Uga. All of the past Ugas are buried around the east end of Sanford Stadium. They have statues with really interesting epitaphs over their graves. They list how many games they won, how many they lost. One of them was named 'Damn Good Dog.'

> There are 50,000 drunken Cajuns running around, cooking everything you can conceive...

One of my fondest memories was in 1978, when Georgia was playing LSU in Baton Rouge. New Orleans was a wonderful Southern town at that time. We left Atlanta on Thursday, got to New Orleans Thursday night, and had all day Friday and Saturday there. On Saturday morning we rented a bus to go to Baton Rouge. If you've never been to Baton Rouge on a football Saturday, you haven't lived. There are 50,000 drunken Cajuns running around, cooking everything you can conceive, all that Louisiana food.

That particular game, Sonny came up to me said, "Will you hold Uga? I've got to go visit for a few minutes." So, there I was standing in the middle of the street, right near the stadium, holding Uga. It was like I was in the middle of a Holy War, with all those drunk Cajuns, who all had those tiger hats on. They'd come up and tease and taunt Uga. He was a big strong bulldog, and he was leaping at them and about to pull my arm out of its socket. Well, that Seiler, damn his hide, it wasn't 10 minutes, it was about 45 minutes before he came back.

In 1965, Georgia was scheduled for the first and only time to play **MICHIGAN*** in Ann Arbor. I had the good fortune to go to that game. This Georgia crowd had more money than God, and they had lined up four taxicabs to go to the game in Ann Arbor, and we fell in with them. We drove up there. The "Red Leader 1," who was in our cab, held a hundred dollar bill in front of the cab driver. He tore it in half and said, "You get me up to Gate 7 and go around the barricade, and I'll give you the other half of that hundred." That cab whipped around the cop standing there, drove us right up to the gate at The Big House. It was a great expense to go to that stadium.

Michigan had won the Rose Bowl in 1964. Their captain was Tom Cecchini. He was touted to be an All-American. Vince Dooley had brought great defense, a Southern tradition, to Georgia. In his last year at Auburn, the Tigers had a great defense. Back then they had AP and UP polls. AP wouldn't recognize them as champions because they were on probation. Michigan was the much bigger team, but it was like a replay of the Florida-Ohio State game in 2007. Georgia was almost twice as fast but very small compared to Michigan. Georgia won 15-7. Can you imagine the euphoria in the state of Georgia? Vince Dooley had beaten Alabama and went and beat Michigan. Man, this state was on fire. Following that Michigan game, Dooley was able to talk Georgia's

*The **MICHIGAN** fight song, "Hail to (the Victors)" was written in South Bend, Indiana in a house where the College Football Hall of Fame is now located.

Governor Carl Sanders, from Augusta, into authorizing the building of an athletic dorm at Georgia, which was called McWhorter Hall. McWhorter had been a Georgia All-American back in 1913. ...

BEAR BRYANT* brought his Texas A&M Junction Boys to Athens for the first game of 1954. They showed up wearing white uniforms, white pants, white tops. Of course everybody wore high-top shoes. Georgia was a heavy favorite. Bryant showed up with 20 players. He didn't even have 22 players. The Aggies were tagged as 'weak sisters,' but proved to be anything but. The Dogs put together only 85 yards in total offense against the underdogs from Lone Star country. Only Harold Pilgrim's fine punting held down the score. Bryant had a kicker who could kick that damn ball 60 yards. He'd kick it. Georgia would drive down inside the 20, and A&M would stop them. He'd kick it back to Georgia. Georgia would drive down to the 20. They won the damn game 6-0, and that was one of Bryant's first games. The Junction Boys were the skinniest, scrawniest little boys you'd ever seen in your life. But, boy, could they play defense! I mean—they were disciplined. The whole game you hung on by the threads.

*The only two schools that **BEAR BRYANT**'s teams played at least three times and never defeated were Notre Dame and Alabama. Bryant coached against Alabama when he was at Kentucky and Texas A&M.

IF YOU'RE LUCKY ENOUGH TO BE A BULLDOG FAN YOU'RE LUCKY ENOUGH

Franklin S. Horne, Jr.

Horne, 62, attended UGA from 1963 to 1968 and went on to serve in the Georgia House of Representatives. He lives in Macon.

In 1965, Bear Bryant came into Athens with his defending national champions. Alabama was whipping the Dawgs. It was in the waning seconds of the game, and like a lot of folks in the stadium, I was disappointed and was leaving the stadium. I was going back to the fraternity house to pour myself a toddy...maybe more than one. My future fiancée and I were at ground level, right behind the hedges on the north side of the stadium and right behind the Alabama bench, when we heard a thud. It sounded like a collision between two football players. I looked out on the field and saw the football in the air. It looked

> I was going back to the fraternity house to pour myself a toddy... maybe more than one.

like somebody had made a good hit on our man, Pat Hodgson, and jarred the ball loose. I thought Alabama was going to recover and run it in for another touchdown, since they were on the Georgia end of the field. Little did I know that it was a designed play, the famous flea-flicker that everybody remembers. Bob Taylor, our tailback, ran a sweep around the end. He pulled the ball out of the air and commenced to running down the sidelines. He ran the entire length of the field for a touchdown. I think that put us a point behind. We completed a two-point conversion and beat them by one point. It was a great day in Georgia football.

Georgia's poet laureate, Agnes Bramblett, wrote a poem about the occasion.

> Up from the bleak, black depths of defeat
> The battling Bulldogs rose to their feet.
> And, snubbing their noses at fate so fickle,
> Turned the mighty Tide into a trickle.

Next, we went up to Michigan and beat them. We may have kicked four field goals that day. It got that season off to a rollicking start. I remember people in Athens the night of the Michigan game went berserk. Jim Martin was a Sigma Chi, the fraternity next door to mine, Phi Delta Theta. The Sigma Chi's had used a plywood football player in their homecoming display. After the **MICHIGAN*** game, Jim and I got that football player and paraded up and down the center of Lumpkin Street with it. Everybody was blowing their horns at us just tickled to death that we had beat Michigan. It wasn't long, though, before the blue lights of the campus police came up. They gave me and my friend citations for disorderly conduct, and we were sober as a judge. Soon we were appearing in Dean William Tate's office on that infraction. He levied a small fine on us, and that was all that became of it. Jim and I later served in the Georgia legislature together.

Some of my fraternity brothers and I have gone to away games together. We went to the Georgia-Florida game thirty-something straight years, through Georgia, through law school and after I got out of law school. The year **STEVE SPURRIER*** was the star

> ***MICHIGAN** and Notre Dame rank 1-2 in victories and winning percentage. The Wolverines have won 860 games. Neither Michigan or Notre Dame has ever beaten Appalachian State.

> *Gatorade was developed a the University of Florida when **STEVE SPURRIER** was playing there. Florida was the first team to ever drink Gatorade. Spurrier refused to drink it, preferring Coca Cola instead. The genesis of Gatorade started when an assistant Florida coach asked "Why don't players pee after a game?" Gatorade was developed on a budget of $43 and garnered the University of Florida over ten million dollars in royalties....In 1966 Florida had all 26 gallons of Gatorade stolen enroute to the Georgia game. Florida led 10-3 at halftime but lost 27-10.

Florida player, Florida had Georgia down 10-3 at halftime. My wife, Pat, my fraternity brother college roommate, Zeke Roots, and his future wife, Joanne, had gotten to the game to find our tickets had been duplicated. I raised Cain with the ticket authorities in Jacksonville, and they found us four seats behind the Florida band near the goal line on the north end of the stadium. Georgia came back the second half and beat Spurrier and the Gators 27-10. Steve Spurrier is one of the best things that ever happened to college football. To hate him is to love him for what it means to the SEC. It just about killed Spurrier that he lost to Georgia that day. That's the year he won the Heisman.

Anyway, after the game there we were, just Georgia fans sitting in the Florida section (they divide the stadium in half—half blue and orange, half red and black...and the two don't mix very well). Everything around us was orange and blue. We had on our red and black. We were yelling because Georgia had pulled a great victory over Florida. Charlie Casey, an all-American at Florida the previous year, was coming down the steps. Casey appeared to have imbibed quite a bit that day. He and his friend stopped beside me as they were leaving the stadium Casey stood 6'4" or 6'6". He was a big man. We were all cheering, "Yea Georgia. Go Dawgs!" When he saw my Phi Delta Theta pin on my wife's sweater, he leaned in my ear. I was trying to ignore the guy. The last thing I wanted was get in a scuffle, get arrested and spend the night in jail. I kept ignoring him, but he shouted louder and louder in my ear. He said, "I don't care if you are a brother in the bond, I'll stomp your _ _ _." At that point, his friend, who had not had as much as to drink as Casey had, pushed him, and Casey stumbled down the steps. It was all he could do to stay on his feet. As we were leaving the stadium, I saw the police putting Charlie Casey, or somebody who could have been Charlie Casey's twin brother, in the back of a police car. I believe it was the same guy who about busted my eardrums a few minutes earlier.

Back in the day, it was a long trip from Cordele to Athens. All the roads were two-lane. It was a full day—we left early and got home late. We tailgated. We would visit friends and family from around the state. Athens was a great place to have a mini-family reunion. We used to have 30-40 people in our party. It was like a church dinner on the grounds. My parents took us to Athens, to Grant-ville for Georgia-Georgia Tech games and to Jacksonville for the Georgia-Florida games.

> ...the Florida fans were...blowing their horns... giving us 'the signal.'

One night we were coming up I-95 from Florida. We had lost the game. As the Florida fans were heading north, they were blowing their horns at us and giving us 'the signal.' We would pass them and when their headlights were on our rear window, there would be two or three shining fannies smiling at them. The only time we did that was when we lost. I don't remember anybody getting mooned when Georgia won.

FLORIDA—THE LAST REFUGE OF SCOUNDRELS

Chris Carr

Carr, 35, is a UGA '95 and '99 Law graduate from Dunwoody, Georgia. He works for Senator Johnny Isakson and lives in Arlington, Virginia.

When Herschel Walker was playing, I thought he was the greatest thing in the world. There I was, a little kid, always diving over the back of the couch like Herschel would go over the top. My dad took me to my first game when I was nine. Herschel was still at Georgia. He made a long run down the sideline and the place just went nuts. I'll never forget it. I've never heard a noise like that—the way the people were cheering for Herschel that day as he was tearing down the sidelines. It was amazing—one, to have your dad take you to a football game, and two, seeing the guy you idolized out there on the field break such a long run and hearing that crowd. It was amazing to a nine year old kid.

I just despise the Florida Gators—the first time I went to Jacksonville was in 1991 and then again in 1992 when Garrison was a front-runner for the Heisman Trophy. We lost that game on a 4th and 12 quarterback draw by Shane Matthews who's one of the slowest men in America...but he picked up the first down. At the end of the game, we were sitting in the end zone, the one nearest the river. All, or most, of the Florida players came down to our end zone to do the Heisman pose and were falling down right in front of the Georgia fans. I thought a riot was going to erupt. When I looked over to the sidelines and saw the Florida coaches standing there laughing, I knew they were just a classless bunch of people—just to see that was the kind of program they have. From that point on, I have always despised Florida.

> There I was, a little kid, always diving over the back of the couch like Herschel would go over the top.

The first game Eric Zeier ever played in was Clemson in 1991. That day, the Braves had clinched the pennant. It was a night game on national television. Zeier was starting. Clemson was ranked #5. We were in the student section. I was in Beta Chi fraternity. It was my sophomore year, and I had just pledged in the spring of '91 my freshman year, so I was a brand new brother. It was the biggest game in Athens in a while. I'll never forget standing up there in the balcony—up in the deck—looking down on the field. The sun is setting. ...and Georgia beat Clemson on the day the Braves clinched the pennant. The whole stadium is doing the Tomahawk chop. The Dawgs win. It was one of the greatest experiences of my life watching that game. I had a fraternity brother who wrote for *The Red & Black*. He had written a column talking about how Clemson thinks they had a football history, but they really don't. He was from Spartanburg, South Carolina. His family got death threats. They put that article up in the locker room as locker room fodder. It's on the Internet to this day. The weekly note to that game was all the attention he got personally and his family got and that article got, and then the Braves clinching the pennant, and then the Dogs beating Clemson on national television when they were that highly ranked, it was one of the best Georgia games I've ever been to.

Herschel is on the President's Physical Education Commission so he comes by our office when he's in Washington, takes the time to take pictures, signs footballs, meets with everybody, and you can sit there and just talk football with him. Two years ago when he was here, Senator Isakson asked him, "I heard about this guy, Matt Stafford, coming out of Texas, and I know you live in Dallas. Have you ever seen him?" Herschel said, "I'm telling you. I have seen him, and he's one of the best high school quarterbacks I have ever seen in my life." To be able to sit there and talk and listen—he talked about Thomas Brown, as one of the best running backs he's ever seen. It's fascinating. Herschel pays attention to the program. He's still close to the program. We couldn't have a better ambassador for the University of Georgia and Georgia football than Herschel Walker.

When we went down to play **FLORIDA STATE*** in the Sugar Bowl a few years back, there is something about being a Georgia fan going to New Orleans and just seeing red and black going up and down Bourbon Street. The stuff we had heard about from the eighties, but never had a chance to experience...I tell people I went to Georgia '90 to '95, during the great depression years. We didn't get a chance to go down to New Orleans, but to be able to go back in 2002 to see the red and black, to feel the excitement in the air, to watch Musa Smith break one and score a touchdown. That kind of stuff was great.

Hey, Larry Munson
Thanks a Million
You Were Great!!!!!

*Lee Corso held the **FLORIDA STATE** record for career interceptions until Deion Sanders broke it. Corso's teammate and roommate at FSU was Burt Reynolds.

YADA, YADA, YADA

My wife Cassie and I have a rivalry that dates back to our college days. I graduated from the University of Georgia in 1992. My wife went to Georgia Tech. We go to the Georgia-Georgia Tech game every year. Some years we sit together. Some years, we've chosen not to sit together. It just depends on where we get our tickets, and whether we're playing at Georgia or at Georgia Tech. Both of us have had run-ins with the opposing team's fans at different games. When the games are at Georgia Tech, quite often we get tickets in the Georgia Tech section through my wife's ties with Georgia Tech. One year, I sat right in front of the wife of Georgia Tech's defensive coordinator, a former player named Ted Roof. She was very, very passionate about her team. We were surrounded by Georgia Tech people. I was the only one in the area wearing a red shirt. She said, "Boy, you picked the wrong seat to sit in today," when I sat down in front of her. Georgia put 48 points on the board on her husband's defense, and she was very upset. Every time I cheered, she yelled at me to sit down. Unfortunately, Georgia Tech scored 51 points that day and won the game 51-48, but I had a long afternoon of verbal abuse from her until the end.

> She said, "Boy, you picked the wrong seat to sit in today," when I sat down in front of her.

Home Depot ran a house-divided contest for people to write in their story of living in a split household. I wrote about growing up having a split family and then marrying into the same situation. We won! Home Depot came out to paint our house. They painted half the house red and black. They painted the other side—the right side—old gold and dark blue to represent the Georgia Tech colors. They did a good job. I called it tactfully tacky. It was pretty gaudy, but, at the same time, it was such a professional job, it actually looked pretty good.

We were in Mississippi the night before the Mississippi State game and a bunch of Georgia fans got into a heated argument over the question: If the Soviet Union were to play the Florida Gators in football, who would you root for? Most of the people were pretty adamant about rooting for the Soviet Union. It was clear we were not going to root for the Florida Gators. The discussion got very intense. One or two people were arguing that you always root for the conference and therefore you have to root for the SEC even if it's the Gators. But the rest of us couldn't pull for the SEC in that scenario. It *was* the Florida Gators, after all, and we had to root for the Soviets under those circumstances. Keep in mind that this argument occurred the night before the Mississippi State game and not the Florida game. Says a lot doesn't it?

—PAUL TEMPLETON, 38,Sandy Springs, Georgia

I lived in Five Points, which is a historic part of Athens on South Milledge Avenue. When I was in junior high and high school, I sold football game programs. My best friend, Tom Headlee, was the pledge trainer for our high school fraternity. We would get all the pledges from the high school fraternity and give each of them 100 programs and say, "You can either go out and sell them and bring us two bucks per program—or give us $200—whichever you want to do."

As a result of selling programs, we got into the Georgia games. The coolest thing that ever happened was the year Georgia beat Alabama with the famous flea-flicker play. I was sitting in the end zone, about 15 feet from where that happened. Bear Bryant, I am told, had a picture of the infamous knee on the ground in his office until he died. I never saw it, but people who knew Bear Bryant told me that was the case.

—RICK BEACHAM, 57, Marietta, Georgia

The tennis program really got started when I was at UGA. Every tennis home match would have 3,500 people there. This goes back to the late '60s, early '70s. The current tennis coach, Manuel Diaz, was a member of the team in the early '70s. He was an electric, charismatic player, and he had a lot to do with creating that turnout. He was like Ille Nastase, very flamboyant. He was always getting the crowd juiced up. They had tennis grandstands built, and they kept adding on and adding on. You had to show up two hours early for a home tennis match and stake out your position.

Dan Magill was the coach back then. The state-of-the-art complex we have now at Georgia is named for Coach Magill.

I remember going to a match in the early '70s after it had become the premiere program in the SEC. We weren't really on a national level with the West Coast schools. Stanford, the #1 team in the country was coming in to play a regular season tennis match. That was very unusual on a tennis budget. The atmosphere was charged, like at a football game. It was even over-the-top for a Georgia tennis crowd. Stanford kicked the _ _ _ _ out of us, but Diaz beat their #1 player in a singles match. That was really all we cared about. Anything that happened after that was going to be gravy.

—<u>RICK FRANZMAN</u>, UGA '75

I was in my third year of law school at Mercer when I went to the 1976 Florida game with a Florida graduate and friend from Mercer. He wanted to make a bet on the game, and we finally decided $5 and the winner would get the right to kick the loser in the rear end at the next student bar association meeting. I can't remember who was favored in the game—I'm sure it would have been Florida because they always were back then. I went to the game, and we were losing at halftime and not looking real good. During the second half Florida chose to go for it on fourth down when they were on their 30-yard line. Somebody made the tackle behind the line of scrimmage and we got the ball back and beat them. That was probably Ray Goff's best game. The Florida fans scurried back under their rocks, as they tend to do when they lose. Howard very manfully owned up at the next student bar association meeting. I was allowed to go up on stage, take his $5 and give him a gentle, but firm, kick in his rear end. That was the best five bucks I ever won. Money won is far sweeter than money earned.

—<u>RUSTY GUNN</u>, UGA '74, Athens native

The 2004 Georgia-Florida game was funny because my niece had just gotten married in Hawaii. None of the family, not even the parents, were there. A family friend, who is not a football fan, planned a dinner party for them after they returned and scheduled it on the evening of the Georgia-Florida game. My wife and I were invited. I told my sister I would be there and said, "You make dang sure he's got that television on the ball game." We left our house at the end of the third quarter so I'd miss as little of the game on TV as possible. I had the game on the radio while we were driving over—about a 10-minute drive. Fortunately, his brother, who is also a big Georgia fan, was there. We were watching the game but Chad, the family friend, had planned the meal for right at six when the game was in it's waning minutes. Georgia had the lead and Florida had the ball. They began saying the prayer for the meal. The game was still on. I had one eye open watching the game while the prayer was going on. I admitted to it afterward. I told them all what I had done because I'm a little bit irreverent.

> I had one eye open watching the game while the prayer was going on.

—JOHN BARNETT, 50, football coach, Thomson, Georgia

From 1916 through 1958, all Georgia Auburn games, except the '29 game, were played in Columbus, Georgia. We lived in Tifton, Georgia, and my daddy, a former minor league baseball player, was a big sports fan and loved Georgia football. In 1922 he had plans to go to the Auburn game in Columbus with friends but my mother was pregnant at the time and my father was concerned that the baby was due. My mother told him not to worry and go on to the game. He went to the game that Saturday afternoon, November 4th and unfortunately, Georgia lost the game 7-3. My daddy came on home after the game and at 2:30 am Sunday morning, I was born. In my opinion, the weekend was not a total loss.

We attended the Sugar Bowl game in New Orleans on January 1, 1981 and Leroy Dukes, a friend of mine from Athens, had invited me to come visit him before the game and have a drink with him in his box. My son and I had no idea where the box was but we went off looking for it anyway. We found a flight of stairs and climbed them and went through a door and into a box. There was a man in the box wearing a dark suit with a telephone in his ear and he came over and said to us, "What are you men doing in this box?" I told him that a friend, Leroy Dukes, had a box and we were looking for him. The man said "This is President

Carter's box, you gentlemen go back out the door you came in!" I just laughed and said to him "You guys aren't doing too great a job of guarding the box cause the door was wide open" and he just gave me the derndest look and my son grabbed my sleeve and pulled me through the door and out of the box like we were instructed. I later read that President Carter's plane arrived late and he didn't get to the game until midway through the first quarter.

In 1965 **ALABAMA*** came to play the Bulldogs in Athens. Late Friday afternoon, the day before the game, my friend Candler Meadors and I went over to Sanford Stadium to watch the Alabama team go through a work out. We were standing on about the forty yard line watching the Alabama team and someone pointed out Coach Bear Bryant. He was standing alone under the goal posts with his arms folded leaning on one of the posts. I looked over at him and said, "He don't look all that mean to me!" Well, I've been told that my voice carries, in fact, my wife often tells me to be quiet in church cause everyone can hear me. Anyway, a few minutes later he straightened up and started walking down the sideline toward us. He passed right in front of us, and when he did, he turned to Candler and me and said, "Well I am!"

—CLAUDE WILLIAMS, JR. UGA '44

In 1991, Georgia was invited to the Poulan Weed Eater Independence Bowl in Shreveport, Louisiana to play Arkansas. I thought that was a big deal until I saw the stadium which was little more than a high school field. At game time, I was on my way up to the press box and got into the elevator with Vince Dooley and his wife and a couple of other people. It was a long slow ride and the elevator was totally silent and I just blurted out, and I don't know why, "I guess I'm the only one in the stadium that actually owns a Poulon weed eater" Everyone in the elevator just looked at me...and the silence was deafening! Georgia did beat Arkansas 21-15.

I was going down to cover the Georgia-Florida game in 1980 in Jacksonville, and all my photographers at that point in the

*Florida State coach Bobby Bowden was a freshman quarterback at **ALABAMA** before transfering to Howard, now called Samford.

season were burned out and wanted to skip a game. I needed an assistant and brought a photographer with very little football experience to assist on the field. I was covering one side of the field and he covered the other. I stayed on the side where most of the action was. It was late in the game and we were behind and it was looking bleak for Georgia. Buck Belue goes back to pass and I got a bunch of good shots of that end of the play but he completes the pass to Lindsey Scott and I hoping that my assistant would get the other end of the play. But, just in case, I went over to the bench looking for a photograph. When Lindsey and Buck met at the bench they were hugging each other and celebrating. There were hundreds of photographers there that day but I was the only one in the bench area. I took lots of shots of the celebration at the bench. Well, when I developed the film I found that I had a pretty good shot and I called the wire service and offered the photo. They said send it in and I did. I didn't hear much but later, one of the Jacksonville photographers came up and was using my dark-room, and he saw the photo on the wall. "Who took this?" he asked. I told him that I did and he said, "You had a lot of people upset in our newsroom in Jacksonville, because we had eight photographers on the field and we ran your photo on the front page of the sports section!" Man, that sure made me feel good!

—WINGATE DOWNS, 47, award-winning sports photographer

I went to school at UNC and never attended a football game. Sure, we'd party on football weekends, but none of us actually went to a game. Basketball was the thing in North Carolina. Then I became a football fan when I lived in Colorado during the John Elway years. I went to many games and they were thrilling. Not so much the game, but the electricity in the stadium and the energy of the fans.

I didn't feel that kind of fan craziness again until my brother took me to a University of Georgia game while I was visiting him. I didn't even know what tailgating was. When we arrived on campus, all my brother's neighbors had set up tables with all kinds of foods and drink. The parents and their kids, now Georgia students, were there and it was so impressive and, yes, heartwarming to see all of them partying together and sharing the same excitement and anticipation of the game. The kids really enjoyed having the parents join them...you don't see that kind of thing much anymore.

When the time arrived for the game and we entered the stadium I could not believe the incredible atmosphere. The stadium was on fire, all in black, and the band was sitting just below us playing their hearts out. The students were going wild and so were their parents and just about everyone. It was one big, happy party with a capital P. One player on the Georgia team, Knowshon Moreno, was wonderful, and I almost went hoarse cheering him on, along with 85,000 other people. It was something I will never forget, not to mention our team won...I wish I had gone to school at Georgia!

—PAT SMEDLEY, Sedona, Arizona

"...all the way back to the hotel, saying, "I love my Bulldogs!"

I went to the Sugar Bowl in New Orleans when Georgia won the national championship. We just knew that we were going to win. I remember my friend Bob had a few drinks that day, going back after the game, all the way back to the hotel, saying, "I love my Bulldogs! I lo-o-o-ve my Bulldogs." He did it over and over and over all the way back. He was so thrilled that we had won that game.

For me going to Georgia was just fun. College was the first time I'd spent four years in one place. It was a special time for me, making friends and getting to go to the games and to the Sugar Bowl and the Liberty Bowl. Back in those days, the Cotton Bowl was one of the major bowls and we got to go there during what was a truly, truly wonderful time.

There's a friend I work out with at the YMCA sometime who is a big Bulldog fan. I was asking him about following the basketball team. He said, "No. To me there's only two sports—spring football and fall football." That's all he likes—the Georgia football part of it.

—RAYMOND PATRICIO, 62, Savannah

TO BE CONTINUED!

We hope you have enjoyed *For Georgia Fans Only.* You can be in the next edition if you have a neat story. You can e-mail it to printedpage@cox.net (please put GEORGIA in the subject line and include a phone number where you can be reached), or call the author directly at (602) 738-5889. The author can't type, has never turned on a computer and has never seen the Internet, so if you need an immediate response, use the phone rather than e-mail.

In addition, we'll be putting together other SEC fan books, so if you have a great story about another SEC team, e-mail that as well to printedpage@cox.net (please put SEC in the subject line and include a phone number where you can be reached).

Note: There were no actual Georgia Tech fans harmed during the making of this book.

Other Books by Rich Wolfe

Da Coach (Mike Ditka)
I Remember Harry Caray
There's No Expiration Date on Dreams (Tom Brady)
He Graduated Life with Honors and No Regrets (Pat Tillman)
Take This Job and Love It (Jon Gruden)
Been There, Shoulda Done That (John Daly)
Oh, What a Knight (Bob Knight)
And the Last Shall Be First (Kurt Warner)
Remembering Jack Buck
Sports Fans Who Made Headlines
Fandemonium
Remembering Dale Earnhardt
For Yankees Fans Only
For Cubs Fans Only
For Red Sox Fans Only
For Cardinals Fans Only
For Packers Fans Only
For Hawkeyes Fans Only
For Browns Fans Only
For Mets Fans Only
For Notre Dame Fans Only—The New Saturday Bible
For Bronco Fans Only
For Nebraska Fans Only
For Buckeye Fans Only
For Georgia Bulldog Fans Only
For South Carolina Fans Only
For Clemson Fans Only
For Cubs Fans Only—Volume II
For Oklahoma Fans Only
For Yankees Fans Only—Volume II
Tim Russert, We Heartily Knew Ye

Questions? Contact the author directly at 602-738-5889.

Sample Excerpts From This Book

…We can be winning by 42 points, and Larry says, "Well, they've got a chance to come back. We've got to keep them down." He has that pessimistic outlook. He keeps us in check, so we don't get too cocky. Vince Dooley was like that, too….

…Clint Eastwood got down on the floor and was wrestling with Uga. Then, Mr. Eastwood looked up at my wife and said to the dog, "Uga, I'm going to make you a celebrity." Cecelia said, "With all due respect Mr. Eastwood, Uga's already a celebrity."…

…I was sitting on the train tracks one Saturday afternoon. We'd been begging, borrowing and stealing booze from everybody around us. One guy volunteered to go if somebody would loan him a car. I had never seen the guy before. In a moment of clouded judgment, I handed him the keys to my car, told him where it was parked and what it looked like. We gave him money and told him to get us beer. He left and that was the last we saw of him….